Our Coal and Iron Industries, and the men who Have Wrought in Connection With Them. The Wilkinsons; With Portrait Of John Wilkinson, "The Father Of the Iron Trade," and Descriptions Of the First Iron Vessel and First Iron Bridge, Wilkinson's Invention Of

THE LATE JOHN WILKINSON,

From an oil painting presented to the Town Council of
Wolverhampton by his relative, Mr. Stockdale.

Our Coal and Iron Industries,

AND THE

MEN WHO HAVE WROUGHT IN CONNECTION WITH THEM.

THE WILKINSONS;

WITH

PORTRAIT OF JOHN WILKINSON,

"THE FATHER OF THE IRON TRADE,"

AND DESCRIPTIONS OF THE

FIRST IRON VESSEL AND FIRST IRON BRIDGE,
WILKINSON'S INVENTION OF HOT BLAST,
HIS WEALTH, ECCENTRICITIES, &C.

BY

JOHN RANDALL, F.G.S.,

Author of "Old Sports and Sportsmen," "The Severn Valley," &c.

WITH A FOREWORD AND APPENDIX.

MADELEY, SALOP:
Printed by J. Randall, "The Salopian and West-Midland Monthly Illustrated Journal" Office.

BARROW-IN-FURNESS:
Reprinted by the Barrow News & Mail Limited.
1917

INDEX OF CONTENTS.

APPENDIX.

Gilbert Gilpin—Letters to the Wilkinsons—Engages under T. Botfield of the Old Park—His Improvements in Pit Chains and Cranes—Medal and Purse of 30 Guineas awarded by the Society of Arts—Advantages of the Invention—Gilpin's Tokens—His Singularities, &c.— Benjamin Edge Invents the Flat Chain with Wood Keys.

FOREWORD TO THE PRESENT EDITION.

This little work, dealing with the life and work of John Wilkinson, " Father of the English Iron Trade," was written by the late John Randall, F.G.S., and published by him in 1876. So far as is known, there are to-day very few copies of the work now extant. Two are known to be in the Barrow-in-Furness district, and, possibly, there are one or two other copies to be found elsewhere.

As the pioneer of the British iron industry, and, indeed, of the iron industry of the world, it has been thought by those responsible for the re-publishing of this volume—kind permission for which has been accorded by the Misses Randall, daughters of the author—that the name of John Wilkinson should be kept in remembrance by all interested in that industry, especially in a district like Barrow-in-Furness, in which district John Wilkinson spent some of his early days and where his remains were interred.

Further, when the developments which have taken place in the iron trade—as demonstrated by the war in which Europe is now engaged—are considered, does it not seem but just that some historical record should exist of the early days of that industry, and of the man who built the first iron boat and erected the first iron bridge ?

And what could be a fitter memento of that period than a record of the life and work of the man who, in an age of doubt and suspicion, stood practically alone, faced and overcame enormous difficulties, bringing to bear method and system to the developing of the iron industry, which in turn has led to the mighty progress achieved up to this present and from which humble beginnings the world is richer to-day ?

The late Mr. Randall's work is reproduced in full, the only changes being the addition of some illustrations to give pictorial value to the record. The original book contained the photo of John Wilkinson, reproduced from the portrait presented to the Wolverhampton Town Council, of which that authority has courteously permitted reproduction again for this re-issue. There was also a photograph of Wolverhampton Town Hall, which has not been included here. In its place there is given an illustration of Castle Head, Grange-over-Sands, which John Wilkinson built as a residence, and in the grounds of which his remains were interred. There has been added the illustration of the Iron Monument which now stands near the foot of Lindale Hill. The other illustrations were in the first edition.

It may be stated here, as an addenda to the work itself, that the eldest daughter of John Wilkinson married, in 1821, William Legh, of Hordley, Hampshire, and became the mother of the first Lord Newton of Lyne. The second daughter married Alexander Murray, of Palmaise Stirlingshire. The only son entered the Army, and subsequently took up his residence abroad.

F.A.Y.

News and Mail Ltd., Barrow, 1917.

THE MAYOR,

ALDERMEN, AND TOWN COUNCILLORS

OF THE

BOROUGH OF WOLVERHAMPTON.

GENTLEMEN,

As representing a Town which owes both
wealth and importance to the Trade of which
John Wilkinson is sometimes said to have been
the father, and as custodians of his Portrait, a
copy of which you have been kind enough to
allow me to use, it occurred to me that I might
fittingly dedicate this little sketch to you.

I do so with great pleasure, from a knowledge
of the fact that, although your ancient Town
came late into the possession of its present privi-
leges, you have in your Corporate capacity con-
ferred great advantages, by the erection of public
buildings, by street improvements, and by the

establishment of institutions, such as the Free Library and others, calculated to promote social mental, and moral improvement—efforts which received timely Royal recognition by a visit from Her Majesty,—a visit which the public spirit of one of your civic members has made memorable by a series of costly illustrations, in connection with a work of art which may be said to be perfectly unique.

I have the honour to be,

Gentlemen,

Your obedient Servant

JOHN RANDALL.

INTRODUCTION.

Our knowledge of the early history of these important industries, even in those places where they have flourished most, is but fragmentary. In the years 1315, 1380, 1392, 1418, and at subsequent dates, references are made in old grants, registers, and documents of various kinds, to coal, to the working, carriage, or use of coal; and from other incidental references to the same subject, as well as from the number of old levels and square shafts discovered at various times, it is evident that coal mining and iron making were industries carried on to no insignificant extent in the fourteenth and fifteenth centuries.

Leland, who in the course of his travels came to South Staffordshire, tells us that "Sea coles abound near Wolverhampton and Wydesbyre"; and that these were worked when Camden was collecting materials some years afterwards for his great work is clear from his statement that "South Staffordshire hath coles digged out of the

·earth, and mines of iron," although he adds, " but whether to their commodity or hindrance I leave to the inhabitants who better understand it."

The reprints, by subscription on the part of the English and Welsh ironmasters, of Dud Dudley's " Mattallum Martis," in 1851, and again in 1854, together with the treatises of Simon Sturtevant and John Rovenson, afforded a fair insight of later stages of our coal and iron industries. The latter treatises first appeared in 1611 and 1613, but the authors, who used high-sounding phrases, and many incomprehensible terms, seem to have accomplished little, practically, compared with what Dudley and others did afterwards. It is clear, however, from their patents and writings, that mineral fuel was being looked to as a substitute for wood, the increased demand for which, for purposes of iron-making and iron-refining, was fearfully reducing the ·amount of timber in the country.

The object the author of the first treatise sought to accomplish by his patent may be gleaned from his preface to the reader, in which he says the principal end of the invention is " that the woods and timber of our country might be saved, maintained and preserved from the great consumption and waste of our common Furnaces and Iron-milnes which as they are now ordinarily built and framed can burne, spend and consume no other fewell than char-coale. The which devise if it may be effected accordingly (as I make no doubt but by God's blessing I shall) will proove to bee the best and most profitable businesse and invention that ever was known or invented in England these many years.

"For (to speak nothing of the great benefit and profit which may be raised and made by twenty other inventions comprised and comprehended under the patent) the yearly vallew of this mettle-businesse alone will amount virto 330 thousand pounds, per annus after the second or third year as appeareth by this calculation.

"A calculation shewing how the mettle invention or art, which maketh all kinde of mettles or metalique substance, with Pit-coale or Seacoale, will be worthy per annum 330 thousand pounds, immediately after the first two years, which are the allotted times for tryalls and conformities without any charges (except the charges of tryalls) to the patentees, partners, assistants and dealers. There are planted already in England and Wales, eight hundred milnes for the making of Iron, for there are four hundred milnes in Surry, Kent, and Sussex, as the townsmen of Haslemore have testified and numbred unto mee, there are also 200 milnes in Wales, and 20 in Nottinghamshire, as the author hath been credibly informed.

"Now wee may well suppose that all England, Scotland, and Ireland (besides the fore-named

Shires) will make up the number of 180 milnes more, being in all 800 milnes Moreover one milne alone spendeth yearly in char-coale 500 pound and more, as diverse clarks, and workmen in iron businesse have credibly testified which in pit-coale will be done with the charges of 30, or 40 pounds after the inventioner's manner and invention or at the most with 50 pound where carriage is farre and chargeable.

"So that the invention in the 800 Iron-milnes will save and gaine—declaro—the owner sof those milnes 320 thousand pounds yearly over, and above their ordinary and annual gaines, as it appeareth by this proportion

" One milne alone saveth yearely	} 400 li {	Ergo 800 milnes save yearly 320 thousand pounds

"Againe the said metallique invention, beeing put and converted to lead, tinne, copper, brasse, and glasse mettle, in all the severall mineralls of England, Ireland, Scotland, and Wales, will questionlesse cleare yearely, by means of fewell, above ten thousand pounds more ; over and besides the ordinary gaines in the said businesse. So that the yearely Iron revenues, added unto these other metalique revenues, doe amount unto 330 thousand pounds, as was said before."

It is clear from this that although a successful substitution of coal for charcoal, first in the making, and secondly in the working and refining of iron, is claimed at dates long subsequent, that its use for both purposes was at that time in contemplation,—a fact which becomes all the more clear if we take the author's description of the fineries and chafferies by which he proposed " to melt, cleanse, and fine the mettals." The patent, dated 29th February, 1611, was for thirty-one years, but the patentee seems altogether to have failed in carrying it out ; and becoming outlawed the very next year, 1612, John Rovenson, who seems to have been a more practical man, and to have profited by the failure of the former, succeeded in having the patent transferred to himself.

It is more than probable that Rovenson prepared his coal by coking it, for he says :— " Fourthly there can be no doubt of performing the matter propounded if the inventor can but make or cause Sea-coale to become as serviceable for metallique purposes as wood and charcoale is. The art and skill whereof consisteth cheifly in three points : The first is to bring earth-coale to that equallity of heat that wood or char-coale hath ; That is to say, that it make neither hotter nor coulder fier than the wood or char-coal doth : The second meanes is so to order and prepare pit-coale, that all malignant proprieties, which are averse from the nature of metallique substances, may be extrated from it. The third means is the addition and infusion of those deficient proprieties, which as they are in char-coale so ought they to be found in pit-coale."

How completely Rovenson, as well as Sturtevant, failed in his endeavours is thus set forth by Dud Dudley, who says .—

" Now let me shew some Reasons that induced me to undertake these Inventions, after the many failings of others, well knowing that within Ten miles of *Dudley* Castle there to be neer 20000 Smiths of all sorts, and many Iron works at that time, within that Circle decayed for want of Wood (yet formerly a mighty Woodland Country).

" Secondly, The Lord *Dudley's* Woods and Works decayed, but Pitcoal and Iron Stones, or Mines abounding, upon his Lands, but of little Use.

" Thirdly, Because most.of the Coale Mines in these parts, as well as upon the Lord *Dudley's* lands, are Coals, Ten, Eleven, and Twelve yards thick ; the top or the uppermost Cole, or vein, gotten upon the superficies of this Globe or Earth, in open works.

" Fourthly, Under this great thickness of Coal, is very many sorts of Iron Stone Mines, in the Earth, Clay, or Stone earth, like bats, in all four yards thick ; also under these Iron mines is severall yards thick of Coals, but of these in an other place more convenient.

" Fifthly, Knowing that when the Collieries are forced to sinck Pits for getting of ten yards thick of Cole one thick Part of the Coles or more, that be gotten under the ground, being small, are of little or of no use in that inland Country nor is it worth the drawing out of the Pits, unlesse it might be made use of by making of Iron therewith into cast works or Bars.

"Sixthly, Then knowing that if there could be any use made of the smal-coale that are of little Use, then would they be drawn out of the Pits, which coles produceth often times great prejudice unto the Owners of the works and the work itself, and also unto the Colliers, who casting of the smalcoles together, which compelling necessity enforcing the Colliers so to do, for two causes ; one is to rise them to cut down the ten yards thicknesse of coles, drawing onely the bigger sort of cole, not regaiding the lesser or small cole, which will bring no money ; saying, *He that liveth longest let him fetch fire further* · Next, These Colliers must cast these coles, and sleck or drosse out of their wayes, which sulphurious small cole and crouded moyst sleck heat naturally, and kindles in the middle of those great heaps , often fals the coleworks on Fire, and flaming out of the Pits, and continue burning like Ætna in Cicily or Hecla in the Indies."

On obtaining his patent he found that he had all kinds of difficulties to encounter in carrying it out. The elements themselves seemed to conspire against him, for he further adds :—

" The year following, the grant or Patent for
making of Iron with pitcole or Seacole, There
was so great a Flood, by rain, to this day, called
the great May-day-Flood, that it not onely ruinated
the Authours Iron works, and inventions ;   but
also many other mens Iron works ;   and at a market
Town called Sturbridge in Commitate Wigorniœ
although the authour sent with speed to preserve
the people from drowning ;   one resolute man was
carried from the Bridge there in the day-time, and
the nether part of the Town was so deep in Water
that the people had much ado to preserve their
lives in the uppermost rooms in their Houses.

" My Yron works and inventions thus de-
molished, to the joy of many Iron masters, whose
works scaped the Flood and who had often dis-
paraged the Authours Inventions, because the
Authour sold good Iron cheaper than they could
afford it ;   and which induced many of the Iron
masters to complain unto King James, averring,
that the iron was not Merchantable ;   As soon as
the Authour had repaired his works and inventions
(to his no small charge) they so far prevailed with
King James, that the Authour was commanded
with all speed possible, to send all sorts of Bar
iron up to the Tower of London, fit for making of
Musquets, Carbines and Iron for great Bolts, fit
for Shipping, which Iron being so tryed by Artists
and Smiths, that the iron masters and Iron-
mongers were all silenced until 21st of King James :

At the then Parliament, all Monopolies were made Null, and diverse of the Iron-masters endeavouring to bring the invention of making Iron with Pitcole, Seacole, Peat and Turff, within the compasse of a Monopoly ; but the Lord Dudley and the Authour did prevaile ; yet the Pattent was limited to continue but Fourteen years ; after which Act the Authour went on with his invention cheerfully, and made annually great store of Iron, good and merchantable, and sold it unto diverse men yet living at Twelve pounds per Tun ; I also made all sorts of cast iron Wares, as Brewing-Cysterns, Pots, Morters, and better and cheaper than any yet were made in these Nations, with Charcoles ; Some of which are extant to be seen by any man (at the authours House in the City of Worcester) that desire to be satisfied of the truth in the invention.

" Afterwards, The Author was outed of his works and inventions before mentioned by the Iron-masters and others wrongfully, over long to relate ; yet being unwilling his Inventions (having undergone much charge and pains therein) should fall to the ground, and be buried in him, made him to set forward his Invention again, at a Furnace called, Himley Furnace in the County of Stafford, where he made much Iron with Pit-cole, but wanting a Forge to make it into bars, was constrained for want of Stock to sell the Pit-Iron unto the Charcole Iron-masters, who did him much prejudice, not onely in detaining his stock, but also disparaging the Iron : Himley Furnace being Rented out unto Charcole Iron-Masters.

" The Authour Erected a new large Furnace on purpose, 27 foot square, all of stone for his new Invention, at a place called, Hasco Bridge, in the parish of Sedgley, and County of Stafford ; the Bellows of which Furnace were larger then ordinary Bellows are, in which work he made 7 Tuns of Iron per week, the greatest quantity of Pit-Cole-Iron that ever yet was made in Great Brittain , near which Furnace, the Author dis-covered many new Cole-mines 10 yards thick, and Iron-mine under it, according to other Cole-works ; which Cole-works being brought unto perfection, the Author was by force thrown out of them, and the Bellows of his new Furnace and Invention, by riotous persons cut in pieces, to his no small pre-judice, and loss of his Invention of making of Iron with Pit-cole, Sea-cole, &c.

Undismayed, however, he applied for a new patent, " into which Pattent, the Author, for the better support and management of his Invention, so much opposed formerly at the Court, at the Parliament, and at the Law, took in David Ramsey, Esquire, Resident at the Court ; Sir George Horsey, at the Parliament ; Roger Foulke, Esquire, a Counsellour of the Temple, and an Ingenious Man ; and also an Iron Master, my Neighbour, and one who did well know my former Sufferings, and

what I had done in the Invention of making of
Iron with Pit-cole, &c.

The new company however were opposed by
old patentees, Sir Philibeard Vernat and Captain
Whitmore, against whom they petitoned the king,
who referred the dispute to Mr. Attorney and
Mr. Solicitor General.

The author then says :—

"Not long after the Wars came on, and caused
my partners to desist, since which they are all
dead, but the Author, and his Estate (for his
Loyalty unto his late Sacred Majesty) and Master,
(as by the Additional Act of Parliament may
appear) was totally sold. Yet nevertheless, I still
endeavoured not to bury my Tallent, but took two
Partners into my inventions, Walter Stevens of
Bristowe Linnen Draper, and John Ston of the
same City Merchant, after the Authour had begun
to Erect a new work for the Inventions aforesaid,
near Bristow, Anno 51, and there were three Partners had in stock near 700l. but they not only
cunningly drew me into Bond, entered upon my
Stock and Work, unto this day detained it, but also
did unjustly enter Staple Actions in Bristow of
great value against me, because I was of the King's
Party ; unto the great prejudice of my Inventions
and Proceedings, my Pattent being then almost
extinct : for which, and my Stock, am I forced to
Sue them in Chancery. In the iterim of my proceedings, Cromwell, and the then Parliament,

granted a Pattent, and an Act of Parliament unto Captain Buok, of Hampton Road, for the making of Iron with Pit-cole and Sea-cole ; Cromwell, and many of his Officers were Partners, as Major Wildman and others ; many Doctors of Physick, and Merchants, who set up diverse and sundry Works, and Furnaces at a vast charge, in the Forrest of Dean."

After many attemps they dessisted Anno domini 1655, and Captain John Copley obtained a patent from Cromwell, but apparently with no better success, and the author adds :—

"Captain John Copley thus failing in his Inventions, An. 1657, he went into Ireland, and all men now desisting from the Inventions of making of Iron with Pit-cole and Sea-cole : The Author, Anno 1660. being 61. years of Age, and moved with pitty, and seeing no man able to perform the Mastery of making of Iron with Pit-cole or Sea-cole, immediately upon his Sacred Majesties happy Restauration, the same day he Landed, Petitioned that he might be restored to his place, and his Pattent obstructed, revived for the making of Iron with Pit-cole, Sea-cole, Peat and Turf, into cast Works and Bars, and for the Melting, Extracting, Refining and Reducing of all Mines, Mettals and Minerals, with Pit-cole, Sea-cole, Peat and Turf ; which said Laudable Invention, the Author was and is unwilling should fall to the ground and dye with him, neither is the Mistery, or Mastery of the Invention Effected and Perfected by any man known unto the Authour, as yet, either in England, Scotland or Wales ; all which three abound with Pit-cole or Sea-cole, and do over-much furnish other Kingdomes many with Pit-cole and Sea-cole, when they might make far better use of it themselves, especially Scotland and Wales, both for the making of Iron into cast Works and Bars ; and also for the making of Steel, and Melting, Extracting, and Refining of Lead, Tin, Iron, Gold, Copper, Quicksilver, and Silver with Pit-cole and Sea-cole."

His petition having been lost, we find him again stating his case thus :—" More cheaper Iron there cannot be made, for the Author did sell pigg or cast Iron made with Pit-cole at four pounds per Tun, many Tuns in the twentieth year of King James, with good profit ; of late, Charcole Pig-iron hath been sold at six pounds per Tun, yea at seven pounds per Tun hath much been sold. Also the Author did sell Bar-iron Good and Mer-chantable, at twelve pounds per Tun, and under, but since Bar-iron hath been sold for the most part ever since at 15*l.* 16*l.* 17*l* and 18*l.* per Tun, by Charcole Iron-masters. More Excellent for diverse reasons, and principally, being the meanes whereby the Wood and Timber of this Island almost exhausted, may be timely preserved yet, and vegetate and grow again unto his former wonted cheapness, for the maintenance of Navigation, which is the greatest Strength of Great Brittain whose Defence and Offence for all the Territories that belong unto it, next under God and his Vice-Gerent, our Sacred Majesties Cares, consists most of Shiping, Men of War, Experienced Marineis, Ordnances, Ammunition, and Stores, the Ordnance made therewith will be more gray and tough, therefore more servicable at Sea and Land, and the Bar-iron will wall, rivet, and hold better than most commonly Charcole Iron. More Excellent, not only in this respect, the Invention of making of Iron with Pit-cole and Sea-cole will preserve Wood and Timber of Great Brittain, so greatly consumed by Iron-works of late. But also in this respect, my Invention will preserve many Millions of Tuns of Small-cole in Great Brittain, which will be lost in time to come, as formerly they were, for within ten miles of Dudley Castle, is annually consumed four or five thousand Tuns at least of small Pit-cole, and have been so consumed time out of mind under ground, fit to have it made Pit-iron with ; which coles are and (unless Iron be made therewith) will be for ever totally and annually lost ; if four or five thousand Tun of Cole be consumed within ten miles compasse, what Coles is thus consumed in all England, Scotland, and Wales ! which is no good Husbandry for Great Brittain, hinc ille lacrime, that our Timber is exhausted."

He then concludes with a retrospect, saying,

xxii.

" Let us but look back unto the making of Iron, by
our Ancestors, in foot blasts, or bloomeries, that
was by men treading of the Bellows, by which way
they could make but one little lump or bloom of Iron
in a day, not 100 weight, and that not fusible,
nor fined, or malliable, until it were long burned
and wrought under Hammers, and whose first slag,
sinder or scorius, doth contain in it as much, or
more Iron, they in that day the workman or
bloomer got out, which slag, Scorius, or Sinder is
by our Founders at Furnaces wrought again, and
found to contain much Yron and easier of Fusion
than any Yron stone or Mine of Yron whatsoever,
of which slag and Sinders there is in many Coun-
tryes Millions of Tuns, and Oaks growing
upon them, very old and rotten. The next invention was to set up the Bloomeries that went by
water, for the ease of the men treading the bellows,
which being bigger, and the waterwheel causing a
greater blast, did not onely make a great quantity
of iron, but also extracted more iron out of the slag
or sinder, and left them more poorer of iron than
the foot-blasts, so that the Founders cannot melt
them again, as they do the foot blast sinders to
profit : Yet these Bloomeries by water (not altogether out of use) do make in one day but two
hundred pounds weight of iron, or there abouts,
neither is it fusible, or malliable, but is unfined
until it be much burned, and wrought a second
time in fire. But some of the now going Furnaces

with Charcole, do make two or three Tun of Pigg
or cast iron in 24 hours. Therefore I do not
wholly compute the vast quantities of charcoles
and wood spent in these voragious works, which
quantity of cast iron, with pit-cole and Sea-cole,
at one furnace I desire not, but am contented
with half the proportion, which once I attained
unto before my Bellows were riotously cut, that
is one Tun in 24 hours ; we need not a greater
quantity, if the like quantity were made in Furnaces in Scotland, and Wales, which abound
with Pit-cole and Sea-cole, as well as England ;
and our supernumery Smiths, Founders, and Forge-
men, and other Tradesmen might be there im-
ployed, thereby to furnish His Majesties Planta-
tions, as well, if not better than England, where
Coles are far cheaper than in England."

Dud Dudley died in 1684, and prejudice and the
old charcoal iron masters once more triumphed,
according to Dr. Plot, who in his "Natural
History of Staffordshire," published two years
afterwards says :—

"The last effort that was made in this country for
making iron with pit coal or coke, was with raw coal,
by one Mr. Blewstone, a high German, who built his
furnace at Wednesbury, so ingeniously contrived that
only the flame of the coal should come to the ore with
severall other conveniences, that many were of opinion
he would succeed in it. But experience, that great baffler
of speculation, showed it would not be. The sulpureous
vitriolic streams that issue from the pyrites, which frequently, if not always, accompanies pit coal, ascending
with the flame, and poysoning the ore sufficiently |to make

it render much worse iron, than that made with char-coal, though not perhaps so much worse, as the body of coal itself would possibly doe."

A " vast amount of coal " however, according to the Doctor, continued to be raised at Sedgeley. Dudley, and Wednesbury, where from " 12 or 14 collery's " were at work, which he estimates at some 7000 tons ; but the wood, he adds, was most of it spent upon the iron works. That prejudice should again triumph for a time, and that " the scythe makers, nail maker's," and others among whom Richard Baxter tells us he laboured, that these whom Dudley estimated at 20,000, altogether should set up a howl of exultation when they saw the last of Dud Dudley and his schemes, considering the failure of many and the partial success only of the few, is not surprising. Their triumph, however, was not of long duration, as the necessity which impelled the experiment every day became more imperative, and a position so gained in advance of primitive and antiquated stages was not likely to be lost, for whoever fails or falls the work of the world goes forward. And, as Dud Dudley died, we find Abraham Darby is born, and from the Wren's Nest, near Dudley, goes to Bristol, and thence to Coalbrookdale where, free to carry out improvements as he thought proper, he takes up the threads of previous experimentalists and, according to his own memorandum book, substituted coal for charcoal in making iron, partially at first, but afterwards altogether in 1812 13. Of the Darbys we propose speaking in connection with the Reynoldses and the Coalbrookdale coal field, the subjects of our present notice being theWilkinsons.   John, of whom we possess most information, and to whom we purpose devoting most attention but of whom so little generally is known was, it will been seen, a man of indomitable courage and perseverence, one who in every way may fittingly be called the worthy successor of Dud Dudley in South Staffordshire, for after a series of four years experiments in adapting his furnace to its new requirements, he succeeded in carrying to a successful issue what Dud Dudley commenced under less advantageous circumstances.

OUR COAL AND IRON INDUSTRIES,

AND

THE MEN WHO HAVE WROUGHT IN CONNECTION WITH THEM.

––––––––––

CHAPTER I.

THE WILKINSONS.

Iron, as Francis Horner once truly observed, is the soul of every other manufacture, and the mainspring of civilised society. It makes the most elastic spring, the largest vessel and the sharpest lancet. In the trembling needle out at sea, as in the last weighty Woolwich Infant, we see the wonderful modifications of which it is capable. The ore, and coal, and limestone used in its production, we term the raw material. And so they are; yet they themselves are the result of processes carried on by nature during the history of past ages, as various and as wonderful as those they now undergo in their passage from the mine to the finished production. There was the wonderful chemistry by which carbonate of lime, set at liberty in one place, was conveyed to a common reservoir in another, there to be modelled into that network of curious forms which constitute the flooring of our coal and ironstone treasures. For the iron ore there were natural castings on a large scale of slag and metal combined. Then, that these may form particles capable of being carried down by the slow-moving machinery of streams into wide expanding lakes, there to form nodules and casts retaining impressions of the living and moving inhabitants of the period, the whole were pounded up and reduced to mud. For coal, laid in beds above and below it, there were employed all the contrivances and intricacies of vegetation upon a wide and extended scale, under conditions of climate, and probably of atmosphere too, which may exist no more On gentle slope and round-topped hill, on wide-extending plain and elevated plateau, one uniform and gorgeous mantle of vegetation spread, absorbing the tropic heat and moisture of the atmosphere above, and the slimy materials below, from which by the usual contrivances of tubes and veins, sap vessels and glands, was produced the solid tissue out of which our mineral wealth was elaborated. As though called into existence for the occasion, some of the many wonderful forms, whose remains can only be found in these subterranean vaults, exist no more. And when numerous generations of these had flourished and decayed, bequeathing their remains to the increasing mass of matter around them, or committing them to the stream, with its rafts and floating leaves, and ferns and reeds, again to be conveyed to some inland sea—the whole had to be compressed, to be overspread and covered, that the gases, struggling amid the process of fermentation to be free, might be imprisoned and bottled up. Who patented the discovery ? Who conducted these wonderful operations so successfully ? Who claims the sigillaria, crossed by the lepidodendron on a sable shield as his family arms ? Truly, the present generation of mankind would have had reason to be proud of the inventor, however far back in the history of the world he may have existed. And shall we feel less grateful to our common Father for the boon ? for who does not amid the causes and results, the agents and the means, interlocking and fitting in, perceive the intervening thread of purpose and arrangement. Whether moulded into hills or fashioned into basins, the earth, wherever pierced by our mines, presents traces of its history that tell at every stage how intimately our present prosperity and happiness are linked and connected with the past revolutions it has undergone. Placed at easy stages below the surface, these minerals stimulate industry. Buried beneath a covering known only to science or experience to indicate their presence, they offer a premium to intelligence, just as in the purposes to which they are applied they task the constructive and artistic faculties. So abundant are the stores, that although the demand may rapidly diminish the stock, it is known that in subterranean chambers, at short distances from those now worked, and separated but by thin partition walls, there yet lie undisturbed in store, elements of wealth for those that may come after, and who may be more worthy of the dower. In the meantime, Nature yields them up with no niggardly hand. On the contrary, she accepts the draught made upon her resources as the standard of worth and energy, and endorses it accordingly. It required a long apprenticeship to learn the true value of the materials, and one almost as long to be able to turn them to account, for it is only within the last few years that they have received such a marvellous development

We have no occasion to go back to times when Roman forges followed in the wake of armies. To that when Wind Furnaces were erected on hill-sides in Staffordshire, or Blow Shops, as that itinerant antiquary Leland calls them, on the Brown Clee, and other hills in Shropshire, for the benefit of a blast. To show the advances made we need not take Simon Sturtevant, John Rovenzson, or Dud Dudley's account of their inventions, although to use a hackneyed phrase, it is at any time " as good as a play " to read " Metallum Martis," and the learned " Treatises " on " Fire Works," and " Protoplast Inventions,', found in that invaluable reprint which Mr Bagnall, of Westbromwich, was fortunate enough to secure a little over twenty years ago. We need go back to periods within our own recollection merely, to modes, processes, and rates of production deemed to be as near perfection as anything human could be at the time, but which seem now to be removed from us by generations and centuries, rather than by years. Take the statement made by a trustworthy correspondent of the *Colliery Guardian*, of August 13th, in which he says that in South Staffordshire at the present time, there are three furnaces that have averaged 820 tons a week for weeks past, or 273 tons each per week, and that there are many whose make ranges from 171 to 230 tons per week each. The average may, he says, be fairly set down at 20 tons a week *more each furnace than it was two years ago.* Why, we remember when, instead of 273 tons, the 73 would have been considered a noble week's work !

John Wilkinson, if we remember rightly—and we think we have his letter to show—was satisfied at one time if he made 20 tons a week. When he first commenced the use of coal at his Bradley works, and raised the production from 10 tons to 20 tons a week, he communicated the fact by letter, dated Oct. 11, 1772, in high glee to his friend and Shropshire agent, Mr. Gilpin ; and he evidently considered that there was some peculiar merit in the coal, for he says : " The coal is got on my estate, and answers well."

John Wilkinson was wont to call himself the " Father of the iron trade," and not without some show of reason, for he is now often spoken of as the founder of the South Staffordshire iron trade. He had the advantage of having been brought up in the workshops of his father, who, as most of us know, was originally a day labourer, working for 12s. per week. Speaking of which he says : " They raised me to 14s. ; I did not ask them for it ; they went on to 16s., and to 18s. I never asked them for the advance. They next gave me a guinea a week, and I said to myself, if I am worth a guinea a week to you, I am worth more to myself." He then set up for himself, but how small a setting up it was may be judged from the fact that when he removed from Cumberland to Furness, in North Lancashire, to make his flat-irons in a shed by the road side, he bought the metal in a liquid state, by the ladleful, from the furnace belonging to the Backbarrow Iron Company, and carried it across the public road to his moulds. The father and two sons, John and William, are described by Mr. James Stockdale, as spending their leisure time in cutting away portions of the large claystone rocks at the rear of the house and foundry to grow wall-fruit upon the surface. It has been said that the two brothers had a sister Sarah, who married Dr. Priestley, but of this we cannot speak with authority.

Subsequently we find the father and his two sons attempting to utilise the rich hematite ores of Furness by means of peat moss dried in the sun, and failing in the attempt. Success, however, followed on the heels of failure ; for John hit upon the happy idea of producing the "box-iron," by which laundresses could more completely gratify the taste of the frilled dandies of the day. These were ground by means of a large grindstone, turned by a waterwheel, which stood on Lindale Beck, at a place called Skinner Hill, close to Lindale village. It was this invention, probably, and the money it won from the fops of the period, that brought the Wilkinsons to Bersham and Bradley. Some time ago we visited Bradley with a view of tracing out these furnaces, if standing, but the result was not very satisfactory. They were the first furnaces, we believe, erected in Bilston parish.

It would often be interesting and instructive if we could put side by side the earliest and latest offerts to accomplish the same end, and this more particularly as regards invention and construction. And this we ought to be able to do in a country which owes its wealth and importance mainly to inventions of the kind ; but the tale of inventive industry is imperfectly known, and what is known is rarely well told Sufficient care, too, is not always taken to preserve the small beginnings of great things.

The two brothers are described as being like

the father, " of a bold, daring, and inventive
turn " ; and they might have been of immense use
to each other, had they held together. But they
quarrelled ; the quarrel culminated in a lawsuit,
and they took independent courses. William went
to France, where he introduced the use of coal for
the first time for making iron. His remarks upon
the facilities possessed by that nation for the
development of the trade beyond anything seen in
that country have been confirmed by those who
have since visited it. " Every provision for making iron," Mr. Wilkinson said upon his return,
" exists in that country, and coal and ironstone
abound. It is England's policy," he argued, " to
keep down the price of iron, so as to prevent them
developing their own resources. Whenever," he
added, " Frenchmen relinquish their fiddling and
dancing, and cultivate the art of iron making, etc.,
England will tremble." This policy may be
sound, or short-sighted, as we consider the interests
of the few or of the many. We introduce the
remarks to show the opinions of the time, and the
correctness of estimates then made and since borne
out by the recent statements of practical men.

James Watt and John Wilkinson Meet.

The meeting of Watt and Wilkinson was a
fortunate circumstance for both, for together they
raised a platform upon which nearly all subsequent improvements have been wrought out.
Watt was struggling in Birmingham, and, writing
to his father that " the fire-engine " he had
invented was going, and answered much better
than any others that had yet been made, and that
he expected the invention would be very useful
to him. He soon found, however, that he wanted

cylinders bored with greater precision than was possible with the tools previously in use. Their irregularities bothered him and frustrated his highest efforts, and he was now on the look-out for a man who could bore them upon a new principle. They met at Bradley to talk over the matter, but it was at the Bersham Works, near Chester, that Wilkinson brought the new boring machine, the merits of which far excelled all previous appliances, to perfection. The instrument used for the purpose of boring previously followed in its progress the inequalities given to the metal by the mould. It guaranteed a circle, but not a straight line ; and Wilkinson by fixing his cylinder and his borer secured both. When Watt returned to Birmingham in 1775, after battling for an extension of time for his patent, he found, as Mr. Smiles says —

" Boulton had been busily occupied during his absence in experimenting on the Soho engine. A new 18-inch cylinder had been cast for it at Bersham by John Wilkinson, the great iron-founder, who had contrived a machine for boring it with accuracy. This cylinder was substituted for the tin one brought from Kinneil, and other improvements having been introduced, the engine was again set to work with very satisfactory results Watt found his partner in good spirits ; not less elated by the performances of the model than by the passing of the Act ; and arrangements were at once set on foot for carrying on the manufacture of engines upon an extensive scale. Applications for terms, followed by orders, shortly came in from the mining districts ; and before long the works at Soho were resounding with the clang of hammers and machinery employed in manufacturing steam-engines for all parts of the civilised world."

The fact is, Watt found in Wilkinson the very man he wanted, and he afterwards frequently resorted

to him for his advice. Eighteen months afterwards we find him applying to Wilkinson for a
cylinder " bored to truth."

WILKINSON SETS UP A FORGE.

Wilkinson resolves to commence the manufacture of wrought iron ; or, as Watt, in writing to
Boulton, described it, " going to work in the forge
way." He was not content, however, with old
appliances, but sent to Watt for a " tilt-hammer,"
which the latter described as " an engine to raise a
stamp of 15 cwts., 30 or 40 times a minute " ;
adding " many of these battering rams will be
wanted if they answer." It answered beyond
expectation.

Wilkinson had not yet begun to use coal at
Willey. His works were in the centre of a well-
wooded country, and charcoal was cheap. He
still used leathern bellows, which were worked
sometimes by a water-wheel, and sometimes,
when water failed, by horses, a man being employed to step upon the top to add his weight to
press them down, and then get off again. In a
letter written to his very able foreman, Gilbert
Gilpin, 1786, he says : " The last bellows we had,
which are now down, were attended with amazing
friction. Some plan on the form of blowing finerys
or chaferys, would do infinitely better for the purpose, and would work with effect when the old
bellows would not stir. I think the wheel used
in stamping, called the Doctors—and now I suppose put to turning—would do better than the
great furnace wheel."

The First Engine Made at Soho.

was one ordered by Wilkinson for his Broseley Ironworks. Mr. Smiles, in his "Lives of Boulton and Watt," says :—

" The first engine made at Soho was one ordered by John Wilkinson to blow the bellows of his ironworks at Broseley. Great interest was, of course, felt in the success of this engine. Watt took great pains with the drawings ; the workmen did their best to execute the several parts accurately, for it was understood many orders depended upon whether it worked satisfactorily or not. Wilkinson's iron-manufacturing neighbours, who were contemplating the erection of Newcomen engines, suspended their operations until they had an opportunity of seeing what Boulton and Watt's engine could do ; and all looked forward to its completion with the most eager interest. When all was ready at Soho, the materials were packed up and sent to Broseley, Watt accompanying them to superintend the erection He had as yet no assistant to whom he could entrust such a piece of work, on which so much depended The engine was erected and ready for use about the beginning of 1776. As it approached completion Watt became increasingly anxious to make a trial of its powers. But Boulton wrote to him not to hurry—not to let the engine make a stroke until every hindrance to its successful action had been removed ; 'and then,' said he, 'in the name of God, fall to and do your best.' The result of the extreme care taken with the construction and erection of the engine was entirely satisfactory. It worked to the admiration of all who saw it, and the fame of Boulton and Watt became great throughout the Midland Counties.

" While Watt was thus occupied, Boulton was pushing on the new buildings at Soho. He kept his partner fully advised of all that was going on ' The new forging-shop,' he wrote, ' looks very formidable ; the roof is nearly put on, and the hearths are both built ' Tools and machinery were being prepared, and all looked hopeful for the future Orders were coming in for engines One in hand for Bloomfield Colliery was well advanced. Many inquiries had come from Cornwall. Mr. ¡Papps, of Truro, was anxious to introduce the engine into that county. Out of forty engines there, only eighteen were in work ; so that there was a fine field for future operations. ' Pray tell Mr. Wilkinson,' Boulton added, ' to get a dozen cylinders cast and bored, from 12 to 50 inches diameter, and as many condensers of suitable sizes The latter must be sent here, as we will keep them ready fitted up, and then an engine can be turned out of hand in two or three weeks. I have fixed my mind upon making from twelve to fifteen reciprocating and fifty rotary engines per annum I assure you that of all the toys and trinkets which we manufacture at Soho, none shall take the place of fire-engines in respect of my attention.' "

Wilkinson found that Watt had given him the very power he wanted to blow his furnace, that Watt's inventions had placed at his disposal a power capable of the nicest, and, at the same time, of the most stupendous operations, a power capable of making his bellows breathe like a zephyr, or blow a blast greater than that of rude Boreas himself ; in fact, that he got the very thing he required for his purpose, for the steam-cylinder suggested to him the plan of producing blast now in use.

It may seem strange to us, living as we do amid the full developments of the power of steam, but it is nevertheless a fact, and one which shows how slow even the keenest sighted men of that day were to open their eyes to the full force of a great truth, that the first use to which the giant power of steam was put was that of assisting, rather than of superseding the old water-wheel. Smeaton's and Watt's engines had to play second fiddles, by pumping back the water over the pool dams, that it might a second or third time prove a motive power to propel the great water-wheels. This was so at Willey, and at the Broseley Works of

Guest, at those of Benthall, belonging to Squire Harris, and those at Coalbrookdale.

Here, for instance, was a stream, as shown in our engraving, and a powerful one, too, coming down from Little Wenlock, near the foot of the Wrekin, which, on entering Coalbrookdale, had to do duty at a series of mills ; first, by turning the great wheel which worked the great bellows, and then, a number of less significant ones, which worked forge hammers, and turned grindstones. Well, the new-born powers of steam were put to the ignoble purpose of throwing the water from the bottom of the Dale back to its respective pools.

According to reports we remember to have been current among old men who knew Wilkinson, but who have since followed the " Great Ironmaster " to his long home, the means he took to possess himself of the Broseley Works were not strictly honourable. These works were in Willey parish, and locally known as the Willey furnaces. Some of the buildings still remain. They may be seen near the lodge gate, by the old drive to Old Willey Hall, and were situated on the estate, and in the centre of the hunting ground of the famous old Willey Squire, George Forester, who, together with his no less famous whipper-in, Tom Moody, Dibdin immortalised in the two songs of " Bachelors Hall," and " You all knew Tom Moody, the whipper-in, well," etc. These works were rented by a company of Liverpool gentlemen, who had spent large sums of money upon them ; but who got little or no return for their capital. Wilkinson, it is alleged, did not intend that they should, for besides keeping a large and increasing stock of charcoal, he had thick iron plates cast to be laid down and buried in the floor, in order, afterwards, to

take them up again. His employers getting no
profits from the works were, at last, glad to
accept of Wilkinson's offer to take them off their
hands. They lay near the outcrop of the coal
basin, so that the mines, being near the surface,
could be worked at any time with little cost ; and
Wilkinson soon made them to pay. He had the
lower coals, such as the clod and little flint coals ;
whilst the ironstones of the district—the pinney-
stone and crawstone, were to be got at the outcrop
in some places, or within a few yards only of the
surface. He surrounded himself with a staff
of able men to whom he could entrust the carrying
on of the works, and as he made a good article he
soon obtained large orders. England then was in
a war fever, pouring out blood and treasure like
water, and preparing to meet the world in arms.
His landlord, Squire Forester, was at the head of
his volunteers, and as member of the loyal borough
of Wenlock, and one who supported the Government of the day in all war-like measures, he
soon obtained orders both from Government
and the East India Company through him.
He had for foreman and manager a very able
man, Mr. Gilbert Gilpin, from whom, through a
friend, we obtained a number of letters, both from
John and William Wilkinson, and copies of his
letters to them. In one of John Wilkinson's to
Gilpin, in the year 1786, we find instructions for
thirty two-pounders, for swivels, for howitzers,
mortars, and shells. He says : " We made some
good strong iron at Willey, from scraps re-melted,
that for *pig only*, I am confident the metal would
not do for guns. For shot or shell it is the best
metal made when melted in these small blasts."

The letter further contains directions for 100 four-pounders, four feet long, and for a number of three-pounders, 3¾. "Aim," he says to his foreman, "at the perfections required by the Board; they will, and do, relax from the great exactings stated; but at any rate they would go down with the East India Company, whose sizes are 8-inch."

From the work at Bersham, guns were sent off to the South for the purpose of being smuggled into France, and at Willey a great number of cast pipes, under the name of water piping, were got up for the purpose of supplying, in reality, the French with good gun metal. These were taken through a woodland country from Willey down Tarbach Dingle, by means of a tramway he constructed, to the banks of the Severn, where all the apparatus for a powder mill had been provided, to be conveyed away from thence for shipping. Shropshire iron, for such purposes as this, had always been in request, and other firms during the war are said to have sent down blocks of iron under pretence of ballast for shipping, which, in reality, were for purposes mentioned above. They were taken down by barges to the Bristol Channel, and smuggled on board French vessels. Some of these pipes were no doubt bona fide transactions. They were for the Paris Water Works; but others it is said were not; and Wilkinson's pipe-making was stopped by the Government, and numbers of pipes remained for years at the warehouse at the bottom of Caughley Dingle.

It was the difficulty of getting barges of the ordinary build to carry his goods down the river which led Wilkinson to construct his

First Iron Vessel.

Compared with the armed leviathans now on the ocean she was a mere Severn minnow; or as a stickleback or a jack-sharp contrasted with a whale; but she was the first, and the precursor of others on the Clyde, the Mersey, and the Thames. She was a notable innovation in her day, and created a wonderful sensation among the barge builders and barge owners. From time immemorial, these winding dales, that owe their creation to streams which man has made to blow his fires and raise his hammers, have been the cradle of iron-making operations. Here, within half a dozen miles of each other, where these natural forces have sawn through minerals they have left standing temptingly out in black and rusty lines along the steep, the first iron rails were cast, the first iron bridge was built, and the first iron keel was laid. Similar circumstances originated and developed the one as the other; and for their present expansion and perfection we are indebted to the suitability and adaptation of the designs to the purposes that called them forth. To carry down to the Severn castings from the Coalbrookdale foundry, the first rails were made; to unite two populous districts—called into existence by the iron works in each, the first iron bridge was built; and to carry down Wilkinson's howitzers, guns, and shells, for the Indian war, the first iron vessel, called the " Trial," was constructed.

Wilkinson could not get barges of wood built fast enough. The barge builders had a monopoly of the trade, and were quite independent, believing Wilkinson could not do without them. Wilkinson said, " I will make an iron barge "; and they laughed at him. He set to work, however, at Willey Wharf, and John Jones—"John O'Lincoln," as he was called, an ingenious smith, of Willey, was foreman. Wilkinson's iron was of the best quality ; and during the spring of 1787, "John O'Lincoln's hammer and tongs were busily plied in riveting and fastening plate after plate of iron , whilst many a joke was cracked by the passer-by, who denounced the innovation in terms embellished by many a round of oaths. Early and late John's hammer was heard—rat-at-tat-tat, rat-at-tat-tat, till the woods echoed back the busy sounds. It was a quiet, sylvan, rural spot where the sturdy smith pursued his task ; and its solitude favoured, as we have said, the exportation of many a bit of good gun iron to the French Government, at the time we were at war with them, in the form of water-pipes—a capture upon the coast by the French cruisers being by no means as objectionable as it seemed.

The summer of 1787 arrived, and a great crowd came down to witness the launch of the first iron barge The woods wore their summer foliage, the sun sent down approving smiles, and the Apley rookery, disturbed by the incursive visitors, furnished a hovering cloud of sable spectators. The plodding ploughman left his task, the artisan his shop, the pedlar his pack, and swarms of sturdy yeomen from vale and upland, dell and dingle, came pouring down to witness the novelty of the launch. "Will she swim ? " "Will she work and prove manageable on the water ? " and "Who will he get to work her ? " were questions that served to occupy the time. Never did son of Vulcan look more proud than John O'Lincoln , if his descent direct from the patron god had been made out and patented he could not have felt more so. A discharge of 32-pounders told that all was ready ; and before the white curling smoke had well died away, the newly-christened " Trial " descended the way-pieces into the river with a splash.

The following is Wilkinson's account of the event in a letter to Mr. Stockdale :—

" Broseley, 17th July, 1787.
" Yesterday week my iron boat was launched ; it answers all my expectations, and has convinced the unbelievers who were 999 in 1,000. It will be a nine days wonder and then be like Columbus's egg "

Wilkinson went on building other barges. In a letter, dated " Bradley Ironworks, 20th October, 1787," he says :—

" There have been two iron vessels launched in my service since 1st September, one is a canal-boat for this navigation—the other a barge of 40 tons for the river Severn. The last was floated on Monday, and is I expect now at Stourport with a lading of bar iron. My clerk at Broseley advises me that she swims remarkably light, and exceeds even my own expectations."

The *Universal Magazine* for that year, vol. 83, p 276, says :—

" November the 8th, an iron vessel, built by John Wilkinson, Esq., was lately launched at Willey Wharf. She is perfectly tight, moves very easily on the water, and draws about eight inches with every accompaniment on board."

The *Gentleman's Magazine* of the same year had, we believe, a similar notice. Others caught up the idea, and iron barges have been common to the Severn ever since. In 1810 John Onions and Son, of Broseley, built a lighter at Brierley, which was sent to Mr. Bishop, of London, in parts, and which was, we believe, the first iron vessel on the Thames. Out of the metallic hills in Shropshire, therefore, came the first iron rails, the first iron barge, and the first iron bridge.

PITT'S PROPOSED TAX ON COAL, IRON, AND COPPER.

When, under Pitt's Administration, it was proposed, in 1784, to lay a tax upon coal, iron, and copper, with a view of remedying the then state of the finances of the country, men like Wilkinson, Watt, and Wedgwood took the alarm. It was a critical period in our history—one when the strong sinews of England were upon their strain, and one when by such acts we may have lost our lead in the race and have thrown into the lap of others advantages our own favourable position and vast mineral wealth afforded. The gravity of the occasion is, perhaps, more evident to us. We can better measure the consequences that must have followed. A tax upon coal would have paralysed trade, checked its development, and with it the means of progress and civilisation. A tax upon coal would be a tax upon iron, upon the manufacture of iron, upon its consumption and its use in arts and manufactures—a tax upon weaving, spinning, and printing,—a tax upon the genius of Watt and Arkwright, whose improvements it would have thrown back and thwarted —upon the extension of commerce at home and abroad. The immense advantages possessed by the manufacturers of the New World would have given them the lead in a race in which, even now, it is as much as we can do to keep up. Our energies would have been paralysed; we should have been deprived of our railways, our locomotives, our steam-fleets, and, probably, of our present unrivalled commerce and prosperity.

Wilkinson by this time, had, it was well known, become a wealthy man; so much so that Telford, in speaking of his appointment by the shareholders of the Ellesmere canal, says, "I had the decided support of the great John Wilkinson, king of the ironmasters, himself a host. I travelled in his carriage to the meeting, and found him much disposed to be friendly." In 1781, too, when Watt and Boulton were struggling with pecuniary difficulties which threatened their position, the former suggested that Wilkinson should be invited to join them as a partner and relieve them of their difficulties; "for rather than founder at sea," he said, "we had better run ashore." It was during that year that Boulton and Watt invented a model steam rolling mill, with two cylinders and two beams, which astonished all the ironmasters, and Wilkinson at once ordered one to be made on a large scale for his Bradley ironworks. He had already ordered a powerful engine, in which Boulton proposed to employ the double cylinder, with double crank, and a pair of fly-wheels, for his Bradley works.

GRAND BANQUET TO WILKINSON AT THE HOTEL DE VILLE.

Wilkinson taught the French the art of boring cannon from the solid. He cast the whole of the tubes, pipes, cylinders, and ironwork required for the great Paris waterworks, the most formidable undertaking of the kind in that day.

He also erected the first steam engine in France, in connection with the Paris Waterworks, on the completion of which the French *savants* gave him a grand banquet. We have his letter somewhere describing with great gusto the event to Mr. Gilpin The lively demonstrations of the French, on seeing the engine at work for the first time, seemed to completely overpower him. He spent a good deal of his time in Paris, and being brought into frequent communication with leading men at that time he was led to adopt " French notions," as they were called, as regarded morals. These tallied with his own views, not only in relation to dogmatic theology but as regarded marriage.

His sympathies with the revolutionary party in France, too, brought him into trouble, together with Priestley and young Watt, in 1793, when the Habeas Corpus Act was suspended, and the King's messengers were making seizures, with the soldiers under arms Watt, after describing what was transpiring around him, says :—

" I hear also that Wilkinson has been threatened with a mob at Bradley, and has prepared to defend himself with cannon, pikes, &c."

WILKINSON'S BUSINESS HABITS.

Many incidents illustrative of character, and many anecdotes suggestive of the mental activity and untiring perseverance with which Wilkinson sought to push improvements in the trade are current. With remarkable vigour of mind, and calm collectedness of purpose, he acted the master of his extensive works Surrounding himself with the most intelligent workmen he could procure, and placing over them agents in whom he could confide, he himself held the reins that governed the whole, and collected from the reports constantly furnished a correct knowledge of his position   By this means he was enabled to bring a mind unfettered by the mechanical details of his concerns to originate and provide new spheres of operations and works of improvement.

Here is a letter written to his Shropshire agent, Mr Gilbert Gilpin, an able and well-informed man, to whom we shall have occasion to refer further on.   Wilkinson loses no time or space by introduction or preface.   His letter is as follows .—

Oct. 2nd, 1793

" I have sent how to take dimensions of Kinman's Furnaces which I intend to enclose.   He is now at work with the smaller in which he melts 1 cwt by a pair of leather Bellows that rises 11 In. 3 foot 3 inches over—& which he says cuts down the Iron fast enough —Says that when smelting Pig Iron 1 cwt will come out not losing above a pound—that where the articles to be cast are small, such as Weights—Bars, Baths, stoves, &c., &c., &c. that there is not any comparison as to be made—& that he never uses an air Furnace but where the metal to be melted & and the articles to be cast are of such size as to require the A. F. :—I tell him that I have been 25 years trying to introduce this plan at difft. times without effect —His reply was that now it will miscarry unless I have a man that has been used to it & likes it.—and that it woud be to my int. to send such a person from hence —this I told him woud be too humiliating a plan for my Agent as well as for myself, independent of the Evills that woud attend such a reformer in the Country

Should any assistance of this sort be wanting I coud get Mr. Picket, or Jas Warring, to come over for a-week. —He is used to these small blasts

The same Machinery with Kinman that turns, bores & scouers—blows his Bellows from a tumbling shaft moved by the Crown Wheel ; a Crank of 5 ft 2 in. moves the Bellows.—the whole to bore, turn, or blow, has nothing but Horses for the power—in many places these small Blasts are worked by Men.

The old mill at Lonsleys—and spare Water there, to Kinman woud be the utmost his wishes could suggest. And all things, Contingencies &c., considered—I am of opinion that woud be the best place for a shot and shell work to use up the stock of scrap—where Moulds—men—Fuel &c.—are quite a diffcrent Matter & woud succeed better unconnected with other work—this is Rule in Town not to interrupt shot or shell with other smaller. But there is another thing I look at—the Esqr. shoud I continue another term—woud rate his old premises £50 per cent more on account of my little additions made in the old work,—tho—they were only temporary.—However—I do not insist upon this—all the scraps might be melted before May—and the furnaces with such Bellows as woud do very well might be removed as readily as other Tools.—It deserves consideration—how far their Branch detached entirely from other work woud succeed better.—there is 20 times the Room and convenience for this Branch at Lonsley that Kinman has—and as to the water it is a mere trifle that would be required to blow two Furnaces of this sort from one pair of Bellows. —Kinman as well as the rest of the Town Founders have repeatedly attempted to melt Gun Borings in those furnaces without any hopes of success.—how far a small portion of rounded Black Lead Slags might answer —may be disclosed on trial—it must be by some additions that Borings can be recalled to a fluid state fit for founders use.

Finally upon this Head.—Shot and Shells being adapted to this ordinary Metal—of which so great a stock is lying dead at Bersham, & the article being now in demand, it appears to be more worth attention than guns on Speculation. Shot, &c., is required annually in Peace by the Co. the price then is low—but in that case I am persuaded it's the only Channel for the Consumption of scraps—as to Borings—they are with me yet a Query.

J. WILKINSON,

MR. G. GILPIN.   Oct. 2. 93.

Mr. Noel Pearce, in a letter enclosing one of Wilkinson's to his father, says :—

" He seems to have been a man of very precise and xact business habits, and rather parsimonious. I have heard, when my father was engaged by him to open out some lead mines at Llynypandu, in Wales, he went to consult him about it, and found him engaged in a loud dispute with his house-keeper over their weekly expenditure, which she could not square up by three-pence ; and my father, when he came to ask for £20,000 towards the mining enterprise, was surprised when he answered promptly : " Well, £20,000 you must have."

The following letter, written by Wilkinson on the appointment of Mr. Pearce's father as his agent at Bradley is characteristic of the man.

Bradley, Oct. 16th, 1798.

Rules for Mr. Pearce.

He is appointed book-keeper, and to examine all payments whatsoever.

The Items formerly drawn out by S. Morriss—need not be done in future—they have not as hitherto executed answered any purpose, but are waste of paper and time.

Mr. Pearce to send J.W. a copy of the cash Payments immediately after they are made—or after pay day—And the following week which preceedes the next Reckoning he is to write Mr. Wilkinson that he has examined the different Books & Items of such cash sent last—& report Errors or remarks that occur to him in such examination—He is also to adopt any better mode that he can devise for rendering the examination of all disbursements whatever clear and distinct—the Items of which as examined must be marked by him & the accouts sign'd—exd. by T. Pearce.

He is expressly requested to note to Mr. Wilkinson on such examination of disbursements or other Payments.—what appears to him that is not clear and perfectory satisfactory, and to point out any method that may make it more so.

Particulars of S. Huttons reckonings will be sent by Mr. Johnson with remarks on the making of Iron &c—But this does not prevent Mr. Pearce's observations on that account so far as his Judgment goes.

He is also to examine the Pottery accounts every reckoning—this does not appear to have been done. These Books to be kept in the Compting House in future—where J. Sefton or any person can make the Entries

Daily —The Mill Books to be kept in lower Compting House—which will be more immediately under the direction of Mr. Johnson, But the Entries from these Books must never exceed one Week ; & be examined as posted by Mr. Pearce, to correct and prevent any Error.

T. Morriss does not appear to be of the least Service, any voluntary attendance in the compting house and what he does there must be under the Eye and direction of Mr. Pearce.

In short Mr. Wilkinson expects from Mr. Pearce a general and it of the cash paid and of all Entries to be made in the Compting House, and finally that he is considered as the Book-keeper and amenable for the correctness of all the accounts—this is Warrant for any interference in the Works where he conceives he can be of service—and from the Weekly Letters being sent Mr. Wilkinson as hereby order'd it is hope some Reform in the accts. will be made at Bradley to the better satisfaction of

JOHN WILKINSON,

Oct. 16th, 1798.

MR. THOMAS PEARCE.

Mr. Pearce's business habits suited Wilkinson admirably, and he remained in his service as his agent thirty years, first at Bradley and afterwards at Hadley, in Shropshire.

In addition to his iron and lead works, Wilkinson, Watt, Boulton, and Wedgewood were large shareholders in Cornish copper mines, where a number of engines had been set up ; but these appear to have been anything but profitable speculations to either of the parties, as may be seen by a letter written by Boulton to Wilkinson, November 21st, 1785, in which he says :—

" Poldic is in a desponding way, and must give up unless better managed North Downs is managed as badly by incapable, ignorant, drunken captains, who hold their posts not by merit, but by cousinship to some of the adventurers."

WILKINSON'S BUSINESS ABILITIES AND SCHEMES.

James Watt had so high an opinion of Wilkinson's businesslike abilities, and of the acquirements and efficiency of his staff at Bersham, that he sent his son, on leaving school, to be in his office. In a letter to Mrs. Campbell, 30th of May, 1784, he says :—

" I have sent my son to Mr. Wilkinson's ironworks at Bersham, in Wales, where he is to study practical book-keeping, geometry, and algebra, at his leisure hours ; and three hours in the day he works in a carpenter's shop. I intend he should stay there a year ; what I shall do with him next I know not, but I intend to fit him for some employment not so precarious as my own "

In 1791, when the steam engine had become, or was fast becoming, an established power, triumphing over windmills, which were stopped by calms, as watermills were by frosts, Boulton wrote in December, saying of the latter :—

" They are all frozen up, and were it not for Wilkinson's steam-mill, the poor nailers must have perished ; but his mill goes on rolling and slitting ten tons of iron a day, which is carried away as fast as it can be bundled up ; and thus the employment and the assistance of these poor people are secured."

Wilkinson was wont to say, " More is done by scheming than by working," and, it is said, when a scheming fit came over him he lay in bed with an iron ball in his hand over a copper basin, so that if he caught an idea and went to sleep before he had worked it out the fall of the ball recalled him to himself. Indeed, it is said that he tried at one time to do altogether without sleep and that after three days' and nights' experiment he was near falling into the liquid iron, and would have done so but that a man rushed forward and saved him.

WILKINSON MADE GAS.

Wilkinson was upon the eve of making a very important discovery—that of making gas. He was, it is said, the first to coke coal in closed ovens for the purpose of extracting an oil ; a process Lord Dundonald afterwards carried on at the Calcutts, near to Wilkinson's works, but whether he or Lord Dundonald was the originator we cannot say. At that time young Cochrane, afterwards Earl Dundonald (the last of our great sea-kings), was a mere stripling, studying chemistry under his uncle, we believe, at the Tuckies, near the Severn ; and it was from such knowledge here gleaned that he propounded to the Government of the day his plan for destroying the Russian stronghold.

A long range of "stew-coal ovens," as they were called, were built for the purpose of driving off the gas and distilling therefrom the tar, about four pounds of which were obtained from every hundredweight of coal. From this coal-tar volatile oils again were extracted, and varnishes valuable for the purposes of japanning. Every gallon of tar thus made has been found to produce half that quantity of volatile oils, while the residuum was equal to the best asphaltum. The process consisted in conveying from the ovens above mentioned the liberated gases, by means of flues, into a capacious funnel built of brick, supported by arches, and covered with lead formed into numerous gutters for the conveyance of water, the chill of which was required to condense the tar. This, falling to the bottom, was conveyed by pipes into a receiver, from thence pumped into a large boiler, and then brought by heat to a proper consistency of tar or pitch. The Severn afforded the means of convenient transit to the coast, from which it was conveyed to the dockyards for the use of the navy, or for other purposes. The gas thus driven off and collected was nothing more than that science has since taught us to turn to account, in lighting up our rooms and streets. It often used to take fire and explode, blowing up the solid masonry around.

The more volatile portion of this tar found in coal, and formed by natural processes, formerly found its way to the surface in what was called the burning well, but which was drained a century ago by the sinking of pits in the neighbourhood. And as further evidence that these natural oils, the result of coniferous plants that contributed so largely to the formation of coal, have been further driven off in large quantities by evaporation or distillation, we may mention the fact that at a short distance from a place called " Tarbach Dingle " petroleum has continued to spring for very many years, and from a tunnel still nearer in much greater quantity, the yield formerly being upwards of a thousand gallons per week. It was collected in a large reservoir and exported. In this case the oils, liberated by the fermentation of the vast accumulations necessary for the formation of coal, became absorbed by the porous sand rock above, which, like a huge gasometer, retained it for ages. When first opened, in 1788, several hogsheads per day were collected.

WILKINSON THE INVENTOR OF HOT BLAST.

Wilkinson also anticipated by many years the introduction of hot blast for furnaces, and that, too, in connection with the plan now followed of re-melting the old slag—an interesting fact which came out some short time since in a trial with the patentee of the improvement. Wilkinson failed, and failed, too, before a difficulty easily obviated. It was customary at that time, as it has been down to a recent period, to use leathern pipes, called bags, for conveying the blast into the *tuyre*, and his hot blast scorched the leather. Such bags, or leathern pipes, terminating at the entrance to the furnace, and protected at the end by an iron nozzle, were, it was deemed, essential to permit the removal of the pipe as the "keeper," or furnaceman wished to regulate his *tuyre*. Long before the hot blast was re-introduced as a discovery, these leathern pipes had been superseded by metal ones, sliding one within the other, upon the principle of the tube of a telescope, so that when the hot blast was again introduced the difficulty Wilkinson felt did not exist. The full merits of this system are now appreciated. It has made available a class of ores before impossible to smelt. It has augmented, vastly, the production of pig iron, and effected a great saving of fuel.

WILKINSON'S IRON MEN.

Wilkinson constructed the first coal cutting machines, or what were called "iron men," for cutting the deeper and thicker coals, then just coming into use. It is said that they answered the purpose for which they were designed, that of

THE FIRST IRON BRIDGE. CAST AT COALBROOKDALE, AND
ERECTED IN THE YEAR 1779. SPAN ONE HUNDRED FEET
SIX INCHES. WEIGHT OF IRON THREE HUNDRED AND
SEVENTY-EIGHT TONS TEN HUNDREDWEIGHT.

cutting the coal on both sides from top to bottom after they had been " holed " under. They were introduced at Bradley and at Broseley, but at both places the colliers refused to " set the trees " to prop up the roof, saying, " If Wilkinson's iron men do the one they must do the other."

THE FIRST IRON BRIDGE.

John Locke has somewhere said that he who first made known the use of iron " may be styled the father truly of arts and the author of plenty." Next to the discoverer of the material, in point of importance, are those who succeed in adapting it to the wants and conveniences of mankind. Wilkinson had a truly prophetic appreciation of the extensive uses to which iron would be applied, and he succeeded in applying it to many new and novel purposes. He had made an iron barge, and he had made an iron pulpit ; he had made iron bellows to blow his furnaces, and iron men to get his coal ; and he was in the habit of saying that the time would come when houses would be built of iron, and when the sea would be navigated by ships made of iron.

Wilkinson had faith in his favourite metal. He believed in iron thoroughly. He never wrote a letter in which he did not mention " iron " either at the beginning, the middle, or the end of it ; and a long time before his death he made an iron coffin for himself, which he kept in his conservatory, with screws and spanner ready whenever they should be required.

When, therefore, it was proposed to put a bridge across the Severn, to connect the Madeley and Broseley banks of the river, at that time two great iron-making districts, Wilkinson at once proposed that his favourite metal should be employed for the purpose. But the thing was pronounced to be preposterous, and Wilkinson was declared to be "iron mad." Both French and Italian engineers had made attempts in the same direction, but had failed, chiefly from the inability of their ironfounders to cast large masses of metal. The first attempt was made twenty years before at Lyons, and one of the arches was put together, but the project was abandoned as too costly, timber being substituted in its stead.

Whether this was then known to the projectors of the bridge we cannot say; the first project was to build it partly of iron and partly of stone, but Wilkinson insisted upon iron, and as he had great influence and was a large shareholder his suggestion was not to be ignored.

The plan the architect suggested was to use part stone and part iron, iron only being brought in to form a sort of crown to the arch; but he had to reconsider his plan, and ultimately adopt the suggestion of Wilkinson, Darby, and others. This bridge, therefore, was the first of its kind, whilst in design and execution, as well as in its span, it was deemed a triumph of skill and engineering unique at that period. Upon old wooden structures, influence by wind and rain, apt to get rickety, and which at every flood raised apprehensions for their safety, it was a wonderful advance. It was no less so upon the heavy, clumsy-looking structures of stone, that impeded navigation, and choked up the stream by their huge abutments.

In 1767 the Shropshire ironmasters had adapted the material destined to become the great agent of civilisation in this and future centuries to the construction of the first iron railways—one of the most useful of all the manifold purposes to which, in this iron age, that metal has yet been applied —while in 1777 they further developed the constructive capabilities of the same metal by raising across the rocky channel of the Severn the first iron bridge, the importance and convenience of which to the district may be imagined from the fact that the town known by its name was called into existence by its erection.

The following will convey some idea of the structure. On the abutments of the stone work are placed iron plates, with mortices, in which stand two upright pillars of the same. Against the foot of the inner pillar the bottom of the main rib bears on a base plate. This rib consists of two pieces connected by a dovetail joint in an iron key, and fastened by screws. Each piece is seventy feet long. The shorter ribs pass through the pillar, the back rib in like manner, without coming down to the plate. The cross-stays, braces, circle in the spandrils, and the brackets connect the larger pieces so as to keep the bridge perfectly steady, while diagonal and cross-stays and top-plates connect the pillars and ribs together in opposite directions. The whole bridge is covered with top-plates, projecting over the ribs on each side, and on this projection stands the balustrade, of cast iron. The road over the bridge, made generally of iron slag, is twenty-four feet wide and one foot deep. The span of the arch is one hundred feet six inches, and the height from the base line to the centre is forty feet. The weight of iron in the whole is three hundred and seventy-eight tons, ten hundred-weight. Each piece of the long ribs weighs five tons, fifteen hundredweight. On the largest or exterior rib is inscribed in capitals : " This bridge was cast at Coalbrookdale, and erected in the year 1779."

WILKINSON'S WEALTH AND INFLUENCE

Wilkinson, as we have said, was now a wealthy and influential man, and his opinions carried weight, not only with brother ironmasters, but with the Ministry of the day, on questions affecting trade. He was not what may be called a public man, being too much immersed in business. He felt, however, to some extent, the responsibilities of his position ; thus, in 1795, which was a year of great distress, in consequence of the scarcity of corn and the dearness of provisions generally, he joined his brother ironmasters, Squire Forester, and other landed gentry, in subscribing for the relief of the poor, and also engaged to deliver a quantity of wheat, under the market price, to the amount of £50. It was one of those times when it would have been dangerous to have held back, for the colliers in Shropshire were only prevented rising and taking what they wanted by force by the ready action taken by such men as George Forester, Richard Reynolds, and John Wilkinson.

In 1787, when, among other schemes, it was proposed to pass a law for making book debts carry interest, the great ironmaster exerted his influence in opposition. He had interviews with Messrs. Banks and Onions, and wrote letters to Mr. Reynolds, Mr. Rathbone, and others on the subject, and raised a powerful opposition to the measure. It was shown that the remedy would prove worse than the disease, inasmuch as the inducement to pay would be lessened on the part of the debtor, who would plead the consideration the law allowed, which consideration would rarely be adequate to prompt payments. Mr. Reynolds, in a letter in reply to Wilkinson on the subject, dated "Ketley, 14th of 12th mo., 1787," put the question in a very fair light by saying :—

" I am against the proposed measure for the following reasons :—At present there is a little, though indeed but too little, regard paid to reputation in the punctual discharge of debts owing : the entitling creditors to legal interest, from the time their debts become due, will I apprehend lessen that inducement to the debtor to pay, and increase the odium unjustly incurred by those, who, however necessary it may be for them, shall insist upon being paid ; because they will be told the law provides for them a consideration and prevents their suffering by their forbearance, though every tradesman knows, as well as the purchasers of land or of government securities, that the interest of money is not at all times, or rather is but very seldom, an adequate compensation for a delay of payment. To renters, whether of mines or works, whose landlords WILL BE PAID, and to manufacturers whose workmen MUST BE PAID, the extension of credit to the purchasers of their produce would be highly injurious ; because it would require an increase of capital incompatible with the circumstances of many of them, as well as increase the risk of bad debts to all, and thereby check the spirit as well as lessen the means of enterprise and exertion, of late years so conspicuously displayed in the extension, and so essential to the continued prosecution, of the various mines and manufactures of this kingdom.

" If it was allowed in cases of bankruptcy, those who had given the longest credit would prove the largest debts in proportion ; but as it would not increase the effects to be divided, I think its only operation would be to increase the number of bankruptcies, by holding out an inducement to the extension of credit, which already contributes so much to a circumstance rendered less scandalous than it ought to be by its frequency."

Mr. Reynolds had cordially worked with Wilkinson, Watt, and Wedgwood, when, as we have seen, Pitt, in 1784, was about to lay a tax on mines. Again, in 1796, when Wilkinson, Reynolds, Crawshay, and others were alarmed by the threat of Pitt that he would lay a tax on coals, to be paid without exception at the pit's mouth, they waited upon the Minister to oppose it. Wilkinson, Reynolds, and their friends, however, found their match in the great Minister, who seemed to know quite as much as they could tell him. Wilkinson was in the habit of laughing, and saying that, besides knowing as much of the iron trade as any of them from experience, he had primed himself with statistics, but that Pitt appeared to know every bit as much about it as he did.

STATE OF THE IRON TRADE.

A paper drawn up for the use of the deputation gives the annual make of Staffordshire iron at fourteen furnaces as $13,210\frac{1}{2}$ tons per annum, and of Shropshire, at twenty-three furnaces, 32,969 tons.

The machinery was for the most part of the most primitive description. We have before us a number of drawings of machines for raising water, and engines by J. Sadler, Adam Heslop, J. Hornblower, Glazebrook, and others, for pumping, blowing, and winding, of 1793, 1796, and later dates. One is an engine without a beam, erected at Wombridge, in 1794, for winding. Another is a blast engine, erected at Hollins

Wood, in 1793. Others are engines erected at Donnington Wood, Horsehay, Madeley Wood, etc., etc.

Some further idea of the state of the iron trade in Shropshire in the latter part of Wilkinson's time may be formed from the following facts, collected at the beginning of the present century.

At Benthall, on the 12th of May, 1803, as we learn from a trustworthy source, there were two furnaces ; one in blast making 30 tons per week of pigs for melting, part of which was used upon the premises, in the foundry : the remainder being for sale. The works at that time were carried on by Harris and Co., and an engine of 30 horse-power, with a single and open-topped cylinder, upon the atmospheric principle, was employed, which could only blow one furnace at a time. The site and some of the buildings at present form part of the works of the Messrs. Maw.

At the Calcutts, 12th of May, 1803 (Alexander Brodie and Co.), two furnaces were in blast ; one making 29, the other 15 tons per week, chiefly of gun iron, which was used upon the premises for guns, mortars, and shell, for Government contracts. A 36 single-power engine worked two furnaces, and a 24 single-power at that date was in course of erection at a short distance from the others to blow a third.

At the Broseley furnaces, sometimes called the " Cunneberry," at others, the " Bottom Coal Furnaces," carried on by Banks and Onions, the make of one furnace was from thirty to thirty-five tons per week, worked by a 20-horse single-power engine.

At Barnett's Leasow, on the 12th of May, 1803 (Wright and Jesson), two furnaces were blown by a 39 double-power engine. The make was about 30 and 35 tons per week, the metal being used principally at their forge, near the Wren's Nest, Apley.

Willey, in 1803, had one furnace blowing—proprietor, John Wilkinson—but the make at the time is not entered.

Madeley Wood, or "Bedlam Furnaces," May 12th, 1803—William Reynolds, proprietor—two furnaces blown by a 50 single-power engine; make at one furnace 20 and the other 30 tons per week; melting pigs, chiefly for sale

Coalbrookdale, two furnaces, Darby and Co., proprietors; make of iron 40 tons at each of the two furnaces, which were blown by a large water-wheel.

The superior production at these works may be accounted for by the fact that a portion of the fuel used was charcoal, that and coke being sometimes mixed for smelting purposes. Nearly the whole of the iron made was used at the foundry. There were also two fineries and one puddling furnace, making bar-iron for their own use.

In addition to the furnaces named, there was at Broseley a furnace called Guest's furnace, a portion of the buildings of which now form part of Mrs. Thorn's tesselated tile works.

At that period the smallness of the quantity made, and the cost of production in the several items of time, labour, and fuel, enhanced the value, and confined the use of iron to few and occasional purposes only. Yet many of the ironmasters then imagined they had arrived as near perfection as possible. The erection of "The Great Blast," the use of the steam-engine, whereby 20 or 30 tons weekly could be made, was indeed a triumph over the foot blasts and "blow shops" which Leland describes upon some of the Shropshire hills, and may well excuse the makers of a century or so since looking complacently upon the revolutions coal and steam had effected.

All the furnaces here mentioned are out of blast. Some have entirely disappeared, whilst fragmentary ruins of others are all that remain to indicate the site.

WILKINSON'S ASSIGNATS AND TOKENS.

In the Hon. George Kenyon's "Life" of his great-grandfather we have the following letter from Whitehall Davies to Lord Kenyon, which refers to the relationship between the celebrated Unitarian previously referred to and the great ironmaster, and which is otherwise interesting :—

"Broughton, Dec. 19th, 1792.

"My Lord,—I take the liberty to trouble your lordship with another letter, in which I have enclosed an assignat, made payable at Bersham Furnace, endorsed Gilbert Gilpin ; I am informed he is the first clerk of Mr. Wilkinson, whose sister married Dr. Priestley. With what view Mr. Wilkinson circulates assignats is best know to himself. It appears to me that good consequences cannot arise from their being made current, and that very pernicious effects may. Mr. Wilkinson, in his foundry at Bersham (where I am informed he has now a very large number of cannon), and in his coal and lead mines, employs a considerable body of men. They are regularly paid every Saturday with assignats.

The Presbyterian tradesmen receive them in payment for goods, by whicn intercourse they have frequent opportunities to corrupt the principles of that description of men by infusing into their minds the pernicious tenets of Paine's ' Rights of Man,' upon whose book I am told public lectures are delivered to a considerable number in the neighbourhood of Wrexham, by a Methodist. The bad effects of them are too evident in that parish."

Of the naughty doings of the Presbyterian tradesmen of Wrexham, and the bad effects of their principles, so " evident " to the writer, this is not the place to speak. but it is interesting to know, from a note in Lord Kenyon's handwriting, that " this letter occasioned the Act of Parliament, passed in 1793, for preventing the negociation of French paper money in England."

The house now in the occupation of the Rev. G. Adamson, of Broseley, was formerly the residence of Mr. Wilkinson, and his offices, which were in the yard adjoining, were broken open and robbed, and a doubt having got abroad amongst the men as to his solvency, he paid every man his wages in his own coin, sending them home with the long and weighty 5s. packets of that period. He issued both tokens of copper, and (in 1788) silver coins of 3s. 6d. each, and also one-pound notes, as other tradesmen of that day did. The copper coins have on the obverse an excellent likeness of him, and on the reverse a forge, steam-hammer, and a workman, and by the side of a pier-head a ship lying, supposed to be the *iron ship*. Some of these coins, however, have on the reverse a ship in full sail. Around the edge of the coins are the words, " Bersham, Bradley, Willey, Sneds-hill, etc."

These tokens or copper pence are referred to in the last line of an old comic song, printed at Oswestry, by J. Salter, and for which we are indebted to *Bye-gones*, published by Mr. Roberts, of Oswestry. It is as follows :—

Ye workmen of Bersham and Brymbo draw near,
Sit down, take your pipes, and my song you shall hear ;
I sing not of war or the state of the nation,
Such subjects as these bring nought but vexation.

Derry Down, down, down, Derry Down.

But before I proceed any more with my lingo,
You shall all drink my toast in a bumper of stingo ;
Fill up, and without any further parade.
JOHN WILKINSON, boys, that supporter of trade.

May all his endeavours be crown'd with success,
And his works ever growing posterity bless ;
May his comforts increase with the length of his days,
And his fame shine as bright as his furnace's blaze.

That the wood of old England would fail did appear,
And hough iron was scarce because charcoal was dear ;
By puddling and stamping he cured that evil,
So the Swedes and the Russians may go to the devil.

Our thundering cannon too frequently burst,
A mischief so great he prevented the first ,
And now it is well known they never miscarry,
But drive all our foes with a blast to Old Harry.

Then let each jolly fellow take hold of his glass,
And drink to the health of his friend and his lass :
May we always have plenty of stingo and pence,
And Wilkinson's fame blaze a thousand years hence.

Wilkinson's Eccentricities and Death.

Wilkinson, like others, had his eccentricities. From a letter before us we find that he had his daughter interred in his garden, we believe, at Bradley, and that he had the body removed five times, and planted a gooseberry tree over it as a substitute for a headstone. The same letter (written by his confidential agent, Mr. Gilpin) informs us that he kept two iron coffins ready in his hot-house, at Bradley, with screws and spanner, one of the coffins being a blank. The following is an abstract from his will, containing his wishes on the subject :—

" And it is my particular request and direction that wherever I die my body may be interred as privately as possible without any parade or pomp, either in my garden at Castle Head, aforesaid, within a place I have there prepared for that purpose, or within a building called the Chapel at Brymbo, or in my garden at Bradley, in such manner as is directed in the book hereinafter referred to, and at the nearest of the said places where I shall happen to die."

The following is his epitaph, copied from his own handwriting, the stars answering, it will be seen, to the letters in his name, the blanks being left for dates, etc., as in the original :—

Delivered from Persecution of Malice and Envy,
Here Rests
* * * *   * * * * * * * * *
Iron Master,
In certain hope of a better State and Heavenly Mansion, as promulgated by Jesus Christ, in whose Gospel he was a firm believer.
His Life
was spent in action for the benefit of man, and he trusts in some degree to the Glory of God, as his different works that remain in various parts of the kingdom are testimonies, of increasing labour, until death released him, the—day of—, 18—, at the advanced age of—.

He died, we may add, on the 14th of July, 1808, aged 80, and was interred according to his directions, at Castle Head, where he had built for himself a residence in Cartmel parish, near the village of Lindale, and where he had formed some beautiful gardens, near what was formerly a small Roman Station. In these gardens, at a place selected by himself, he was buried.

That the evil men do lives after them, and that the sins of the fathers are visited upon the children to the third and fourth generation, often frustrating even their good designs and intentions, are authoritative sayings which seem verified in the case of Mr. Wilkinson. We have preferred to dwell upon his life rather than his death, and upon what he did rather than what he did not do ; but there are some curious and to an extent instructive and interesting facts connected with Wilkinson's end which it might here be proper to add.

He died at his house at Hadley, and his body was enclosed, according to the instructions to his executors, in wooden and leaden coffins, and was taken in a hearse drawn by four horses to Castle Head. In crossing the estuary the drivers got entangled in the quicksands near Holme Island, from which dangerous position horses and hearse were with much difficulty extricated by workmen and others on the estate.

As great difficulties appear to have beset the carrying out of the great ironmaster's clearly expressed wishes as to his interment as afterwards attended the disposal of his property ; and in neither respect were they finally carried out.

In the first place, the inscription on his coffin was altered to please his executors, thus—

"JOHN WILKINSON,

IRON MASTER,

WHO DIED 14TH JULY, 1808,

AGED 80 YEARS.

HIS DIFFERENT WORKS,

IN VARIOUS PARTS OF THE
KINGDOM,

ARE LASTING TESTIMONY

OF HIS UNCEASING

LABOURS.

HIS LIFE WAS SPENT IN

ACTION

FOR THE BENEFIT

OF MAN,

AND, AS HE PRESUMED

HUMBLY TO HOPE,

TO THE

GLORY OF GOD."

In the second place, as we learn from Mr. Stockdale, when the body was brought down to Castle Head, the iron coffin proved to be too small to receive it, owing to the thickness of the lead and wooden ones with which it was encased ; the body, therefore, was temporarily deposited in an adjoining walk until such time as a larger iron coffin could be made at the works in Staffordshire.

In the third place, when the new coffin was brought down, and the body placed in it, and an attempt made to dig a deep grave for it at the place selected, it was found that the rock approached so near the surface of the ground that the huge new coffin could not be put so deep as to place it out of sight. It was thought, therefore, that there was no other way of doing it

THE WILKINSON MEMORIAL AT
LINDALE IN CARTMEL

but again to disinter it, which being done, and the rock removed, the coffin and body were again interred, and a pyramidical *iron* mausoleum, as ordered by himself, of 20 tons weight, was placed over his grave, not 20 yards from the drawing-room windows of the house.

Here the great ironmaster's body rested for about 20 years in peace, but when it was in contemplation (in 1828) to sell the estate, it was thought that the fact of his being buried so near to the residence might injuriously affect the sale of the place, and John Wilkinson's body was a third time disturbed, and carried in the night, in the heavy iron, wood, and lead coffins, up the steep hill adjoining, to the neighbouring chapel of Lindale, and interred under the pew belonging to Castle Head House, where it now rests in peace, after having been four times buried and three times disinterred ; whilst the grand mausoleum itself has been pulled down and taken away.—*Sic transit gloria mundi.*

It appears from a work called " Annales Caermoelenses," written by James Stockdale, Esq., who was a nephew of William Wilkinson, that John Wilkinson kept not only his own but several other iron coffins of various sizes, partially hidden among the laurel and other evergreen trees in his grounds, which he was in the habit of showing to his visitors, to some of whom he offered such iron suits gratis.

Castle Head here referred to, when purchased by John Wilkinson, about the year 1765, was a barren rock, here and there overrun with brambles and brushwood, which the great ironmaster converted from a wilderness into gardens and shrubberies, by soil carried in panniers on the backs of horses. During the rise of the tide it was surrounded by the sea, but it appears to have been selected, probably from the facilities it offered for defence, by some early settler upon the coast, for when Mr. Wilkinson commenced to dig the foundations of his house he came upon a number of early British and Roman remains, which were brought under the notice of Dr. Priestley by his brother-in-law, who, with other celebrities, visited at Castle Head House, and of which he has fortunately left a description They included lead, clay, glass, and brass and stone ornaments , also remains of boars, buffaloes, and other animals ; seventy-two Roman coins, several supposed to have been British, and a number of other equally interesting remains of remote antiquity.

WILKINSON'S WEALTH LOST IN LITIGATION.

Wilkinson died possessed of extensive works and estates at Bradley, Staffordshire, and Brymbo, Denbighshire ; of others in Surrey, Cornwall, Salop, Westmorland, etc., etc. His machinery alone was set down as worth £130,000. Mr. Wilkinson left his mansion, furniture, plate, etc., at Castle Head, together with £500 per annum, to Ann Lewis, a person who had lived with him ; and after providing for trustees, etc., etc., the remainder of his property and estates were to be in the hands of his executors for 21 years, for the benefit of three children, by the above , his wife having died a short time before his death. In the event of the above three children's death, the whole was to go to a nephew, Thomas Jones Wilkinson. The latter, taking advantage of the fact that the children, not being born in wedlock, were not legally entitled, notwithstanding the clearly-expressed will of the deceased, took proceedings with a view to get possession of the whole.

These proceedings lasted seven years, in various courts in the kingdom, the plaintiff gaining every trial till the case was carried before the House of Lords, and finally before the Court of Chancery. Sir Samuel Romilly was engaged for the plaintiff, and old Lord Eldon was Chancellor. After a long trial, the latter sent for plaintiff, before judgment, to inquire privately what provisions he proposed to make for the others if judgment should be in his favour. He was answered, " None," and to the astonishment of the court " Old Bags," as he was called, next day gave judgment for defendant, thus reversing all previous decisions taken upon the law of the case We need scarcely say that by this time the whole affair had become involved, or that finally this vast property accumulated by unremitting thrift and perseverance was frittered away and lost.

Not content with the failure of his attempt to set aside his uncle's will as related to the three illegitimate children, by the decree of the Lord Chancellor, whose verdict was to establish the intentions of the testator, stung too, probably, by throwing away his only chance by his selfish refusal, in reply to the question as to his intention at a private interview with the Lord Chancellor, Jones Wilkinson entered an appeal to the House of Lords. With the aid of a Mr. Bolton, of Birmingham, and a Mr. Ferriday (who had been nominated a trustee under Mr. Wilkinson's will, but which trust he some years before relinquished, 'taking an indemnity), he filed a bill in Chancery and moved the court for an injunction to restrain Mr. Adam, who was the faithful and confidential agent of John Wilkinson during his lifetime from further interfering in conducting the trusts of the deceased's will, on the alleged ground of waste, gross mismanagement, etc. The Vice-Chancellor referred the inquiry to the Master, and after a hearing which occupied 92 folio pages by a short-hand writer, the Vice-Chancellor, as we learn from a letter of Mr. Adam now before us, dated 30th of August, 1819, said :—

" In as much as these affidavits afford to me no proof that Mr Adam has not conducted himself with integrity, I cannot conclude that it will be for the interest of those, who are now, or may hereafter be interested in this estate to remove Mr. Adam," again " If I saw ground to impeach his integrity it would be necessary at once that this court should interfere with a strong hand." " But this is not the view I take of the affidavit, I can well account for the conduct of Mr. Adam from a sincere zeal to benefit the family." He adds, " but the court is to protect the property, and I am not to look at the motives, but to consider the steps necessary to protect the property. If for the benefit of the infants it is fit Mr. Adam should be continued in the management of these concerns, however, indiscreet Mr. Adam's zeal may have been, there can be no reason why the court should not do that which is essential for the property, namely, continue him in the management " On one of the counsel remarking " that the persons bringing this suit are the greatest enemies the children have, and that Mr. Adam is the greatest friend they could have," the Vice-Chancellor observed ; " I am much disposed to agree with you in respect of his conduct," and the Vice-Chancellor afterwards added, " I believe there is no person in the empire capable of managing the concerns but Mr. Adam, that is my belief." He says in another place, " Under such provisions and regulations as are essential with regard to infants property, I must put this (" inquiry ") to the Master, at the same time meaning to remove every imputation from Mr Adam, there is nothing here which affords the least colour for it." The Vice-Chancellor adds in another place, " professing again what is my sincere opinion that there is not a person in the kingdom more fit in point of experience and talent, and in point of integrity."

In reference to persons with whom Mr. Adam had dealt, the Vice-Chancellor observed " I do not propose to interfere with Mr Adam, I might hazard the whole property by doing it, but still it seems to me my duty requires should refer it to the Master whether it will be for the benefit of the persons interested that Mr Adam should be removed from the management of the Trust Property, or continued under what regulations, or provisions, and the Masters to be at liberty to state all circumstances specially," and further in allusion to the effect which might be produced in the country by such reference he added I do not feel there could be any different impression on the country whether the motion stands over —in truth there is no ground for alarm to the country because whatever measures the court take, on the report of the Master will be measures of protection to every person having claims on the property, if Mr. Adam is removed such must be the provisions the court must make, for it cannot remove Mr Adam without protecting all those who have dealt with him, &c."

Jones Wilkinson and Ferriday did not escape the ruin brought upon Wilkinson's three children and their mother, for both became bankrupts.

With reference to Wilkinson's relationship to the famous Dr. Priestley, of Birmingham, referred to in the letter to Lord Kenyon, it does not appear that he was much influenced thereby. On the contrary, we are informed that " the learned theories and scientific investigations of the worthy doctor were scarcely appreciated by the hard-headed, practical, business-like brother-in-law, who could concur so far as ' Matter ' was concerned, but who frequently was heard to declare, with regard to other and less tangible things, that he could ' make nothing of the fellow.' " As a sympathiser with those liberal views on politics and religion enunciated by the learned doctor in his " Familiar Letter to the Inhabitants of Birmingham," and in other ways, he was threatened, as we have seen, by the "Church and King " mob, and had to guard his works from their attacks.

WILKINSON'S SHROPSHIRE COLD-BLAST IRON.

The cold-blast iron made by Wilkinson at the two furnaces he built and carried on at Hadley was so tough that the men had the greatest difficulty in breaking the pigs, frequently having to throw them down from ten to a dozen times to do so. The following agreement entered into between the executors of the Wilkinson estate and Messrs. John Bradley and Co., of Stourbridge, for all iron made at these works for seven years, is perhaps the best testimony .—

" London, March 26th, 1813.—James Adam, on the part of himself and other executors and trustees of the estates of the late John Wilkinson, and John Bradley, of Stourbridge, on the part of himself and James Foster, his partner in business, mutually agree as follows :—

" The said John Bradley, and James Foster, agree to purchase, and the said James Adam agrees to sell the whole of the pig iron made at the Hadley Iron Works, part of the estate, of the said John Wilkinson, for seven years next after the twenty-ninth day of June, in the present year, (1813), on the following terms.

" The iron to be make in the usual way, and as it has been made for these last two years, without any unfair means being used to increase the quantity at the expense of the quality, and the whole of the iron so made to be considered and reckoned as of one quality, whether part of it be melting iron, best forge, or of inferior quality, and charged at five pounds, seven shillings and sixpence, per ton of the usual weights of 120lbs., to the cwt , and twenty cwt to the ton, the said iron to be delivered to the agent of Messrs. John Bradley and James Foster, at Stourport, from time to time in the usual manner as soon as may be after it is made and the weight ascertained, immediately on the delivery, and a receipt for the same specifying the quantity to be given by the said John Bradley and James Foster, or their agents to the said James Adam or his agent. And the said John Bradley and James Foster agree to pay for all such quantities of iron at rate aforesaid, in each month, on the 1st. day of the following month during the whole, and to the end of the said term in good bills of exchange drawn up and payable at London, to the satisfaction of the said James Adam, (viz.) for the first 12 months payable as aforesaid three months after date; and for the remainder of the said term, payable six months after date; and the said parties agree that a more formal agreement shall be drawn up at the expense of the parties when required with the usual clause of settling by Arbitration any difference that may arise in carrying this agreement into effect, and in the mean time the agreement to be binding to all intents and purposes. It is understood that the payments for the first twelve months may be by Messrs. John Bradley and James Foster's acceptances at three months after date, payable in London if no particular objection should be made to the same by the said James Adam. And it is also understood that the usual allowance for sand and cinder shall be made in ascertaining the weight of the said iron. Witness our hands the 26th day of March, 1813.

" JOHN BRADLEY,
" JAMES ADAM."

The following letter from Cornelius Reynolds, of Broseley, to Mr. Thomas Pearce, on his taking the management of the furnaces and colliery at Hadley, will show the small proportions of the materials used :—

" Broseley, March 29th, 1804.

" Sir,

" As I hope by this time you have got the pipes to the hot water pool lay'd down, and the filling apparatus completed, and that some half charges of Top coal cokes have been put into the furnace, preparatory to beginning with mine, I therefore wish on receipt of this to begin immediately, observing the following directions. To every 5 baskets of Top coal cokes, filled as long as the cokes will properly lay on, of if more convenient for wheeling, &c., thus : 6 baskets may be filled a little above level, or the same as when I was over last, for a half charge, to which put

cwt.	qr.	lbs.	
1	0	0	weight of Pinney ironstone
1	0	0	weight of Brick measure ditto
0	3	14	weight of Limestone.

" The ironstone and limestone to be broke small, say about the size of a good egg, the ironstone free from dirt or dust. This quantity to be continued until I come over next. A board should be provided and put up in the bridge house to note the number of half charges put in, which will be useful to know about what time the mine may be expected down.

" I wish it may be well scufful'd every morning and the bars kept in some time to give air sufficient to give life to the cokes, but I wish that process to be deferr'd on Monday morning until I come over, and I intend to be quite as soon as usual.

" I trust any other matters wanted will be put in a state of readiness as much as possible before a beginning is made. A proper shovel for filling the cokes, tools for drawing the cokes, breaking limestone, &c., will be among the necessaries wanted.

" I am sir,
" Yours respectfully,
" CORNELIUS REYNOLDS."

Another letter from the same to John Wilkinson, and his remarks, interlined, touching the Hadley engine and the works at Bersham, shows that they had then begun to cast closed-top steam cylinders at these works, which an old book published at Wrexham, in 1789, thus describes :—

" About four miles from Wrexham is Bersham Iron Foundry, the most considerable one of the kind in Europe ;

it is the property of Messrs. Wilkinson Brothers. Here
engines of mortality of all descriptions are cast, not only
for this kingdom, but for most others,—in the extremest
parts of the earth, the fame of this foundry being loudly
reported."

As a somewhat curious indication of the manner
in which, notwithstanding the vast concerns
in which Wilkinson was engaged, he gave his
mind to the smallest details of matters he took
in hand, we may notice a calculation of his for
supplying his furnace-men at Hadley with ale, in
which he goes into the minutest particulars as to
the quantity of malt, sugar, etc., with directions
where such are to be purchased, the number of
pints which the 201 strikes of the former and
4,440 ℔s. of the latter will make, and what the
grains and small wort will produce.

John Wilkinson and his Agents.

The various able men who managed Wilkinson's
works in different parts of the kingdom appear
to have been impressed by the genius presiding
over them, and a confidence and mutual respect
alike complimentary and honourable to the
parties seems to have existed between them.
Mr. Pearce, as we have seen, was appointed on
his coming over from Cornwall to manage some
lead mines at Llynypandu, near Mold, and his
son, Mr. Thomas Pearce, father of Mr. Noel Pearce,
of Stourbridge, was, as we have seen, installed
manager, first at Bradley, and afterwards at
Hadley, of the ironworks ; and as showing the high
estimation in which his services were held it may be
mentioned that during his last illness Wilkinson
sent for him, and asked him not to leave the concern after his death, but to stay and look to the

children. Mr. Pearce did so, at a disadvantage to himself, and notwithstanding an offer of a partnership in the Lawley works. It may be added that the sons, grandsons, and great-grandsons of the Mr. Pearce who was the agent of Wilkinson at Llynypandu, have continued to fill important offices of trust in large ironmaking firms of South Staffordshire and Shropshire down to the present time.

JOHN WILKINSON'S IRON BOAT.

In " Annales Caermoelenses," previously alluded to, a work we had not an opportunity of consulting till our last sheet was going through the press, we find it stated that the inventive resources of the maker of the first iron barge had led him to construct an iron boat some years before. When the father and two sons were smelting the rich hematite iron ore of Furness with peat moss, they cut a canal through the turbary for the passage of a small boat, to convey the peat to the furnace, and an iron boat was made for the purpose. Mr. Stockdale adds that " there are people still living (amongst them Mr. Nicholas Atkinson, of Cart Lane) who remembers having seen it about seventy years ago."

Mr. Stockdale says :—

" A novel idea had suddenly flashed across John Wilkinson's mind ! a great but simple truth, till then hidden to all the world ! that iron might be made to float in water ! that a heavier body might be made, under certain circumstances, to float in a lighter ! And may it not be reasonably assumed that the building of this small iron boat at Wilson House, in Cartmel parish, furnished John Wilkinson with the idea of building the

much larger vessels he afterwards constructed
in 1787-1788, at Willey, and that *Cartmel* parish
has the high honour of having had the first iron
vessel constructed in it, and that, too, by the one
of its own parishioners! Yes; that this Wilson
House Iron Boat was really the parent of all
the iron ships that have ever since been built—
our noble-sided men-of-war, and that leviathan of
ships, the " Great Eastern " herself, not excepted!
Labor omnia vincit or, as the old English rhyme
has it—

> " By hammer and hand
> All things do stand."

Apropos of this we may add the following,
supplied by Mr. Askew Roberts, from " Bygones " :

"An anecdote is told of a local country blacksmith
who had dropped his hammer temporarily to listen for the
first time, to the relation by a neighbour of the story he
had heard of Wilkinson's intention to make a Canal Boat
of iron ; and who, with the utmost astonishment and in-
credulity, threw into his water-bath the horse shoe he had
been working on, and asked the relator if he thought iron
would swim, when the shoe had sunk to the bottom in a
moment ! "

WATT AND BOULTON'S EARLY ENGINES.

Mr. Stockdale says :—

"My grandfather, James Stockdale, was much connected with both the Wilkinsons and also with Boulton
and Watt, in several large mines in Cornwall and Wales,
viz., Wheel-virgin, Chasewater, Polgooth, Nant y palma,
Myrcyfinnon Wen, Minera, Lanarmon, Stedford, and
others ; and as he was the chief worker of the hæmatite
iron ore mines in Furness after about 1756, at Whitriggs,
Lindal Moor, Coat Close, East Side, West Side, and other
places, and was likewise engaged in carrying on the
furnaces at Leighton and Halon, and the forges at Carke,
Caton and Liverpool, he supplied John Wilkinson, not

only with the hæmatite iron ore, but also with the charcoal-smelted hæmatite iron of Furness. Indeed, on looking over the books of the Carke forge, I find a quantity of this fine iron was sent, on the 21st of May, 1768, to James Watt, of Greenock, then assiduously engaged in perfecting his fire engine. What Watt at last had fully completed and obtained a patent for his steam engine, then called a " fire engine," one of the first of these was constructed for my grandfather's cotton works at Carke, by John Wilkinson, under the personal superintendence of Watt, at Wilkinson's great works at Bersham. It was a pumping engine, as were all Watt's engines at first, and was used for the purpose of lifting the water out of the tail race back into the mill dam, and thus, as it was thought, of furnishing a continuous supply—an operation which had till then been less perfectly performed by a large gin or wheel, turned by six horses. But the engineer of the cotton works soon perceived that to apply the like engine power directly to the works of the mill would be a more economical application of steam power, and this soon afterwards was done, a new and still more powerful engine having been obtained for the purpose. As this first fire engine was then a wonder and a novelty, so it became the sign of the inn at Carke, and a perfect facsimile of this engine of Watt's figured over the door of the inn for eighty years—this inn being called the " Fire Engine " to this day."

Mr. Stockdale says :—

" Mr. Hall, the present owner of this mill at Carke, on sinking a drain, found the well in the tail race, out of which the water was pumped and thrown back into the mill dam. When this fire engine was going at full speed, and the wind was in the south-west, the noise it made was so great that it could be heard to Newton, five miles distant ! This was the case with all Watt's engines at first, and when he was making attempts in Cornwall to put an end to this jarring and noise, the proprietors forbade him, for they said it denoted the power of the engine ! "

THE STREAM WHICH SUPPLIED THE CHIEF WATER
POWER FOR THE GREAT BELLOWS AND FORGE
HAMMERS OF COALBROOKDALE WORKS, WHEN
WATT'S FIRST ENGINE WAS ERECTED.

Mr. Stockdale confirms p. 214, what we have stated on p. 22, that John Wilkinson erected in France (Creuzot), one of " Watt's engines "—the very first ever seen in France. On this occasion he wrote to Watt as follows :—" Crusal, September 13th, 1785. The engine is in operation. The Frenchmen are delighted. It is a complete success, and the numerous visitors, amongst whom were the Duke D'Angoulesne, M. Bertrand, etc., etc., expressed their satisfaction. I wish you had been here." John Wilkinson's opinion was " that the French would soon be on an equal footing with England in the mercantile arts, if that country should turn out to be equally favoured and rich enough in minerals." He about this time contracted for the supply of iron pipes (forty miles in length), necessary for conveying from the river Seine a sufficiency of water for the whole city of Paris—" Paris Waterworks, "the wonder of that day ! This was the work of a company of shareholders, and he not only took many shares himself in the undertaking, but induced many of his intimate friends in England to do the same ; my grandfather, amongst the rest, taking ten shares of 1,200 livres each."

William Wilkinson received £10,000 principal and interest of money invested in these works, as indemnity, after the peace in 1815. Mr. Adam, as trustee of the estates of John Wilkinson received a large sum ; we have understood something like half a million of money. He went over, half fearing that the debt would be repudiated, and was pleasingly surprised to find it discharged to a fraction.

APPENDIX.

We by no means claim credit either for the completeness of our biographical notice of the Wilkinsons, or for the arrangement of the particulars it contains, some of which came to hand after the first sheets were printed, whilst others, interesting as to dates, reached us subsequent to the completion of our sketch.

Thus, from a Biographical Notice of the late John Wilkinson, published by Bridgen, of Wolverhampton, a few years ago, accompanied by a lithographic portrait, kindly lent us by James Walker, Esq., we learn the following facts, which may be of use to future compilers.

John Wilkinson was born at Clifton, in Cumberland, in the year 1728. He removed to Kendal, and was put to school under the Rev. Mr. Rotherham. Having passed through the usual course of education, at the age of seventeen he was apprenticed to a merchant in Liverpool, with whom he continued about five yesrs. In the year 1755 he married a young lady named Mawdsley, by whom he had a daughter of promising talents, who died early. In 1763 he married for his second wife a Miss Lee, of Wroxeter, a lady possessed of a ample fortune. It is stated that in private life he added to the character of the most affectionate of husbands the habit of benefiting the meritorious part of his fellow-creatures, of whatever country, in whatever situation, or of whatever persuasion, and that his property, honourably acquired, and as honourably diffused, was great. In person, Mr. Wilkinson was strongly built, and his voice remarkably deep and sonorous when seventy years of age.

Mr. Wilkinson was of a bold, enterprising, and somewhat arbitrary disposition, and whilst struggling hard in early life to maintain his position as an ironmaster was usually lively, and even facetious, on one occasion a plethoric friend having complained of irresistible drowsiness, saying he could not keep awake, he replied, " Not keep awake ! Put my bill book under your head, and I warrant you won't sleep."

The notice from which we glean the above concludes by saying ·—

" His career was a wonderful one, and the results of his extraordinary genius and perseverance in the iron trade of South Staffordshire, of which he has been denominated " the Father," were acknowledged by all ; while among the lower classes his energy and determination gave rise to uncommon stories ; and it is a fact that a belief extensively prevailed that he would re-visit his works at Bradley after his death. This event, it was reported, was to take place on the seventh anniversary of his decease , and on that day several thousand people assembled on Monmore Green and its neighbourhood, expecting to see him make his appearance, riding, as the tale predicted, on his grey horse ! Such a circumstance clearly betokens the uncommon character of the individual to whose portrait this hasty sketch is an accompaniment."

One of John Wilkinson's agents was Gilbert Gilpin, whose abilities were such as to require a distinct notice, and the more so as his improvements and discoveries led to a recognition of their merits by the Society of Arts, a society founded in 1754 for "The encouragement of the arts, manufactures, and commerce of the country, by bestowing rewards for such productions, inventions, or improvements as tend to the employment of the poor, to the increase of trade, and to the riches and honour of the kingdom," etc. ; a society which has rendered immense service to industrial art, to art workmanship, to the improvement of manufactures, and the spread of technical knowledge, from its commencement down to the present time.

Of the early history of Mr. Gilpin we know nothing. He was the friend of the brothers John and William Wilkinson, and after they quarrelled, when each collected a small army of men with hammers and crowbars to demolish their own works at Bersham, he still remained the friend of both, who were never reconciled, and was the means of keeping each well informed of the other's doings. He was about the best trade correspondent and letter writer of that day, and various letters now in existence on the iron trade of that period supply a great amount of information.

Gilpin left the service of John Wilkinson with a view of beginning business for himself. In his letter, dated 1786, he says, " I must decline your proffered engagement of undertaking some business on the Continent unless it is of such a nature as will enable you to give me £150 per annum, exclusive of travelling charges ; I have no idea that you will give any such salary because there are numbers of persons who will do it for less, and

I must therefore decline as it is my intention as soon as peace takes place to go to France, and either by myself or in company with another to start an iron foundry.

Instead of going to France, however, he went to undertake some marble works in South Wales, where he wrote a number of letters to John and William Wilkinson, the latter of whom was then residing at the Court, near Wrexham ; letters which treat not only of the iron trade but of political and other matters, and are in a chatty, pleasant, gossiping vein, with comprehensive sketches of personages, movements, and industrial operations, of the time when the Crawshays, the Homfrays, Sir R. Salisbury, Sir C. Morgan, and others were the prime movers. He chats with " Tom Guest," " Thompson," and " Old Peter Onions," who, in his eightieth year, he tells us, is still following his clock and watch-making business at Dowlas, and who patented his invention for working and refining iron, and converting the same from a fluid state into bars by applying blast to it in a molten state in 1783. The following is the concluding portion of one of Gilpin's gossiping letters.

" J. W. is expected at Rowley's daily, I have not heard much of his proceedings lately. He has two coffins ready in his hot house, at Bradley, the first being a blank, with spanners, &c., to screw him up. He sent the order from London, and was very pressing for its speedy execution, which made his people conceive the d— had at length sent him his route and passport.

" His daughter was interred in the garden, but he has had her remains five times removed, and at present a gooseberry bush is the substitute for a tombstone. Rowe has left him and has gone into partnership with Mr. Wiggin, or Graham, or both, in a foundry in London.

Meers is gone from Bradley to manage the Ridriff works in lieu of Rowe. Will Rylands and Morris got into his seraglio in the night sometime ago, and the girls (3 in no.) not having full confidence in each other so far as related to keeping the secret, disclosed it, and one of them wrote J. W. respecting it, in consequence of which he wrote Mr. Giles one of his clerks (a seafaring man) to sleep in the house every night, since which Mrs Giles has become jealous of her husband and the ladies of the harem. It is not known how Rylands and Morris will get off when J. W. arrives.————has been very ill, and the same state of warfare is kept up amongst all the people concerned as has been always encouraged at J. W's concerns. A person of the name of Wood, who is collecting materials for the life of J. W. has sent to me requesting anecdotes or other matter respecting him. I could furnish him with much material from notes made a few months before I left his employ, but who knows the use that might be made of them? Wood is a brass founder at Wolverhampton, and I have more than once suspected J W. may have employed him to get such information from me to enable him to do away with the ' old obligation ' he conceives himself under to me.

" A singular circumstance has occurred to William Emery, the nailor of Wellington, and brother to Emery who sold Hadley to J. W. He saw in one of the magazines that a part of an estate in Kentucky was to be sold to defray the taxes, and it was supposed to belong to a person of the name of Emery, in England. As Emery had an uncle who died at Washington, he wrote the Secretary of State for Kentucky stating the circumstance, and a few days ago he showed me the answer which he had from Toulmin the under Secretary, by which it appears that the estate which consists of 226,000 acres is his property, and that they had sent him the forms &c., necessary to be attended to by one of the ships for Liverpool, and which are just come to hand.

" Dear Sir,

" Yours truly,

" G. GILPIN."

Pit Chains.

On leaving South Wales, Gilpin, in consequence
of the high price of ropes, which had greatly risen
from the difficulty of obtaining hemp during the
war with Russia, turned his attention to the improvement of pit chains as a substitute for hempen
ropes for winding purposes.

The steam engine was just then beginning to
supersede horse labour in winding, which had been
accomplished either by a jack-weight drawn down
an inclined plane, or by means of a machine
called a gin. One or more horses were yoked
to cross-pieces of wood in an upright shaft, passing
at the upper end through a barrel sufficiently
high for the ropes to clear the horses' heads.
But the steam engine, or "Sawney" as it was
called by way of derision, was soon found cheaper
and more effective than horses, and capable of
bringing up with much less risk loads from a
greater depth than had yet been ventured upon.
The rope or chain was made to work upon cylin-
drical barrels, or a double cone, base to base ; and
the slipping of one coil, or the confusion caused
by irregular wrappings round the barrel, not infre-
quently caused accidents, to prevent which Gilpin
constructed grooved pullies, turned upon the lathe,
for the links to fit in, and barrels, upon which
were coiled spiral iron "tire," between and
which the chain fell into position, so that each fold
was at an equal distance from the other. "The
Mechanic," a very respectable authority of that
day, says :—" The old oval linked chain, in use for
common purposes from very remote times, had in
it a twist, arising from the weld of the iron. Ropes
used in mining and other operations were apt, by

coiling irregularly, to slip, and consequently to break. To obviate the latter evil in chains, Gilpin caused grooves to be cast in his iron pullies of just sufficient dimensions to receive those links of the chain that work vertically, while those working horizontally, and what may be called the gudgeon part of it, were made to bear upon each side of the grooves. Barrels of cast iron were also provided, with *spiral grooves* of the same dimensions, at such a distance from each other as to admit the chain to *bed, without the danger of a double coil*. By these means the links were retained at right angles with each other, the only position for free and uniform motion. The links of the chains are made as short as possible, for the purpose of increasing their flexibility, and they are reefed perfectly free from twist in the pullies and on the barrels, for the same reason." The paper proceeded to state "That this method of working chains was first put in practice at the ironworks of T. W. and B. Bottfield, near Shiffnal; and employed in the workings of cranes, capable of purchasing from ten to fifteen tons; in the working of the governor-balls of the steam-engines constructed by Boulton and Watt, and in the raising of coal and ore from the mines, for which purpose ropes have before been solely used. The chains, in all cases, have performed with the utmost safety, uniformity, and flexibility; so much so, that the prejudices of the workmen against them are entirely done away, and the heaviest articles are hoisted with more ease and as great confidence of safety as with the best hempen ropes." With a view of ascertaining the relative flexibility of ropes and chains, the friction, and power requisite to move certain weights, a table detailing experiments made with each is given. The paper then proceeds : " Contrary to the general opinion, it also appears that chains are safer than ropes ; for it is an established axiom that those bodies whose fibres are most in the direction of the strain are the least liable to be pulled under, and in the examination of the properties of a rope, we find that the strands cross the direction of the strain in undulated lines, and consequently prevent its uniform action thereon. A rope is subject to this inconvenience, even when stretched in a direct line, but more particularly so when bent over a pulley, as in that position the upper section moving through a greater space than the under one, is acted upon by the whole strain ; and hence the frequent breaking of the ropes in bending over pullies, from the double strain over-loading the strands of which the upper section is formed The links of a chain are subject to the transverse strain, where they move in contact ; but as such strain is in proportion to the length of the bearing, it must be very trifling. All the links have axles of their own, *the chain moves simultaneously with the strain, and both are in consequence retained in continual equilibrio.* A chain in grooves will, therefore, sustain as great a weight when bent over a pulley as it will in a direct line, and, consequently, is safer than a rope. A safe, uniform, and flexible method of applying chains in the working of machinery has long been a desideratum in the art ; or they are but little affected by exposure to the weather, or the heat of manufactories, whilst either produces the speedy destruction of ropes. The discovery is of additional importance, as it substitutes a durable article for a very perishable one, and gives employment to our manufactories at the expense of foreign importations. The durability is at least six to one in favour of chains."

The paper further contains a description of a crane, illustrated by drawings, and then gives an account of improvements of machinery for raising coals, ore, mines, etc. ; also the results of Mr. Gilpin's inventive genius.

The paper, which is clearly and ably written throughout, then proceeds : " Although the method of working chains in grooves had been in use three years and a half at the time this paper was drawn up (1807) and T. W. and B. Bottfield had nearly two thousand feet in daily motion at their manufactory, yet not a single link had broken or the least accident occurred therefrom. The wear was so trifling that it appeared the chains would sooner fail from oxidation than attrition, for although the machines for raising coal and ore from the mines are in use twelve hours in the day, the brown oxide of iron formed upon the links by exposure to the atmosphere is seldom disturbed by the motion of the chain. It is probable, therefore, that in this manner of working, chains will last at least fifteen years ; but to be certain, it is taken at twelve in the subjoined comparative statements, which show that the expense of chain as cordage is not a fourteenth part of that of hempen ropes. And in this statement the superiority of chains is so far from being overrated that there is every probability the expense of them will be less than the twenty-fourth part of the hempen ropes The method of folding wooden barrels with wrought iron tire does away with the necessity of cast iron ones, and may be applied to every wooden barrel now in use at a small expense, as may be seen by the following estimate :—

Statement of the expense of tarred ropes for a machine for raising coal and ore from a pit eighty yards deep, for three years and four months .

	£	s.	d.
Ten ropes, each 110 yards long, 6 inches in circumference, and 5lbs. per yard, 5,500lbs. at 8d. per lb	183	6	8
Deduct 10 worn-out ropes, 2,750lb., at 1d. per lb.	11	9	2
Expense of ropes for three years and 4 months	171	17	6

Expense of chains for the same machine, and for the same time :

	£	s.	d.
Two chains, each 110 yards long, formed of ⅜in. iron, 28 links to the yard, and weighing 5lbs. per yard, 1,100lbs., at 6d. per lb. ...	27	10	0
180 yards of wrought iron tire, with the holes punched therein, weighing 7lbs. per yard, at 1s. 6d. per yard	13	10	0
540 nails for the tire, 27lbs. at 1s. 6d. lb.	0	13	6
Workmanship nailing the tire on the barrel, 180 yards, at 2½d. per yard	1	17	6
	£43	11	0

Gilpin, from his leaving South Wales to this time, had been in the service of the Bottfields, but he now left them in consequence of their objecting to his attention being divided between his duties to them and his chain-making, unless he gave them a share therein, and he now set up for himself. "The Cambrian," in 1814, in an article under the head of "Substitute for Hempen Ropes," says —"Gilbert Gilpin, Coalport, near Shiffnal, Shropshire, sells chains of the best Shropshire iron, which will raise upwards of a ton weight in general use, at 5d.per pound, or 3s. per yard. Upwards of eight thousand yards of pit-chains made by him are now in use in the mines and collieries of the Lilleshall Company, Shropshire, and the adoption of such an immense quantity at one concern is a proof of the efficiency of the article. They are also in use in the principal manufactories of England and America."

Gilpin's improvements in chains were further recognised by the Society of Arts by the presentation of a silver-mounted purse with thirty guineas. On one side was the date "1805," and underneath, "Society of Arts," in gold letters, surrounded by olive branches, whilst on the other were the words, "Thirty Guineas," surrounded by heraldic devices, having "Gilbert Gilpin" underneath.

Besides this pecuniary recognition the society further expressed their approval of the improvement in the then "crisis of public affairs," adding, with regard to the chains, that they are more flexible than hempen ropes, and from their greater durability bear but a very small proportion thereto in expense, that they are applicable to all the common barrels and pulleys now in use, without requiring the least alteration in either.

Gilpin's Trade Tokens and Eccentricities.

Like his former master, John Wilkinson, Gilpin issued trade tokens, both copper and silver, of a very superior class. Around the rim, in a band on either side, is " Gilbert Gilpin, Dawley, Shropshire, pays the bearer a halfpenny," and in the centre is a finely-executed crest of a wild boar, with " 1811 " underneath. The opposite side sets forth that he " sells chains for pits, cranes, etc., of best horse-nail iron, at 5d. per ℔." A silver token from a very superior die, bearing the same inscription, was of one shilling value.

Gilpin was an attentive observer of men and manners, and delighted in sketching character as displayed around him. His former employers, Messrs. Wilkinson and Botfield, came in for some severe critiques from his pen. Provincialisms were chronicled by him in alphabetical order, and a dictionary of the Welsh language was at one time contemplated and commenced. A valuable collection, too, of minerals and fossils was made by him from the surrounding district. Like Wilkinson, too, he rather delighted in being singular. On one occasion, when a gentleman of distinction—we believe someone connected with the Board of Trade—called upon him at his residence, and, after some conversation, invited him to the nearest inn, for the purpose of having a friendly chat, the chainmaker consented, but peremptorily refused to enter the carriage, saying he should not trust himself, " the horses might run away or the thing may break down ; he did not mind a ride in a canal-boat, but he would not risk his neck in a carriage." Both parties proceeded to the " Elephant and Castle," Dawley

Green, the one on foot, and the other in the carriage.

DISCOVERY OF THE FLAT CHAIN WITH WOOD KEYS.

The single-link chains were far from satisfactory, however. Much prejudice existed, in the first place, amongst the colliers, who refused to descend or to come up in them, and who insisted upon a rope being used for the purpose. Nor were matters very much improved till Mr. Reynolds, of Ketley, offered a prize of £50 for an improvement in pit-chains.

The first improvement was the three-linked chain, but the woods used for holding the links together was an afterthought on the part of Mr. Benjamin Edge, who had for some time been making chains at Coalport, where he succeeded the Hortons. While doing some repairs to a three-linked chain, he had occasion to put in a piece of wood to hold it together. The idea struck him that this was the secret of success, and making a piece of chain upon that principle, he showed it to William Reynolds, who at once adopted it, and flat chains with wood keys at once came into general use. Mr. James Edge succeeded to his father's business, and his sons, John and Joseph, still carry on chain and wire-rope-making on an extensive scale.

Messrs. Edge and Sons have in their possession a portion of the first flat chain attempted. It contains iron pins, each pin running through seven links, that is, four and three alternately, of 5-16ths of square iron. The iron of which the links are composed is very irregular as to length, which would, of course, cause the chain to wear untrue, and very irregularly.

Wire ropes have now as completely superseded flat chains as these superseded the old-fashioned-ones of round and oval links ; and these are manufactured now by the firm to a large extent at Madeley and Shifnal, to which places they have removed their works.

It is the boast of the firm that no lives have ever been lost by the use of their chains. From the time their grandfather succeeded in introducing the wood key to keep the links together, somewhere about the year 1810, to the present, they have with slight exceptions continued to use the best Shropshire iron for their chains.

Quite a revolution has been wrought in this kind of manufacture, deeper shafts and quicker speed have led to a demand for round and flat wire ropes of the very best steel and charcoal iron.

This demand for superior wire ! es has increased of late years, not merely by the expansion of mining enterprise, and their introduction as guides, and as capstans, but for steam ploughs, etc. , so much so that Edge and Sons have had to build new works, both at Madeley and at Shifnal, where they now employ extensive first-class machinery.

We may add that Mr. James Edge effected improvements in chains which secured for his father a prize medal in the exhibition of 1851. Also that Mr. William Walton, of Madeley, succeeded to much of the chain-making business formerly carried on by his uncle, Mr. James Harris, who served his time with the famous Gilbert Gilpin.

Lightning Source UK Ltd.
Milton Keynes UK
UKHW02f1835300918
329792UK00004B/67/P